Linking Mission to Money®

Finance for Nonprofit Leaders

SECOND EDITION

Bulk orders of *Linking Mission to Money*°
may be ordered directly from:
LMM Press
471 Highgate Avenue
Worthington, OH 43085

Email info@linkingmissontomoney.com
for price and shipping information.

Cover design: Dustin Verdin
Index by Clive Pyne Book Indexing Services

Library of Congress Card Catalogue Number: 2010913058
ISBN-10: 1453793380
EAN-13: 9781453793381

Linking Mission to Money®

Finance for Nonprofit Leaders
SECOND EDITION

Allen J. Proctor

Author of *More Than Just Money,*
Practical and Provocative Steps to Nonprofit Success

PRAISE FOR THE FIRST EDITION

"Just the section on 'Building a Mission-Focused Budget' would be worth the investment in *Linking Mission to Money*, the best resource for board members I've read in a long time. Principled, informed, mission-focused governance is well served by this indispensable handbook for social sector, nonprofit boards. Thank you, Allen Proctor." *Frances Hesselbein, Chairman, Leader to Leader Institute (formerly known as the Peter F. Drucker Foundation)*

"Proctor's demystifying book is important, and he argues powerfully that while budgets, projections, and fiscal prudence are essential, we must never forget the higher aspirations of our institutions."
Professor Jeremy Knowles, Harvard University, Dean Emeritus, Faculty of Arts and Sciences

"*Linking Mission to Money* is the book we have been waiting for. It takes nonprofit finance and lays it out in a way that is smart, strategic, and straightforward. No one should serve on a nonprofit board without it."
Mary McCormick, President, Fund for the City of New York

"The transition to being a not for profit board member is fraught with uncertainty regarding roles and responsibilities. Allen Proctor has provided the new and experienced board member with a treasure trove of insights on overseeing the financial processes of non profit institutions. A must read for anyone interested in improving governance in the not for profit sector!"
Leonard Schlesinger, President, Babson College

This book is dedicated to my wife Gail Walter,
who makes everything possible

TABLE OF CONTENTS

INTRODUCTION TO THE SECOND EDITION

Since the 2004 publication of the first edition I have been grateful for the positive response to the book and the numerous helpful comments and suggestions from readers and attendees at my seminars. Inspired by this response, I have corrected errors, introduced improved explanations and illustrations, added introductions and key questions to each section, and updated material for events and issues that have occurred over the past six years. I also wanted the second edition to be of value to nonfinancial readers as well as leaders of nonprofits who may not serve on a board. I have, therefore, added an index and an appendix: the first to make it easier to find discussions of specific topics; the second to summarize actions readers might take to lead their nonprofits using the principles in this book.

The second edition retains the goal of the original book: to help nonprofit leaders to be successful by explaining finance as the core of a holistic approach to fulfilling their responsibilities. This broad-based approach aids in linking money to mission, mission to action, and action to accomplishment. It argues that finance is far more than a set of numbers; rather, it can serve as the primary tool to carry out the most important obligation: to know what is going on. The financial picture of a nonprofit can be painted in a way that is understandable to everyone who is responsible for the strategic direction of a nonprofit. Like any specialty, finance can either be made complex or be made understandable. If it appears complex, the people responsible for the organization's finances—including board members—may not understand the situation well enough to make it understandable.

The approach to finance described in these pages will help all nonprofit leaders to participate equally and fully in financial reviews and deliberations and fulfill their duty as fiduciaries. Fiduciaries have the legal responsibility, and personal liability, to know what is going on at their organization. Each is individually accountable for the organization to adhere to its mission, spend its money in line with that mission, and attract sufficient resources to remain financially viable. Pablo Eisenberg of Georgetown University, a frequent contributor to the *Chronicle of Philanthropy*, described board accountability succinctly: "Nonprofit boards are the first and last line of defense against poor performance, corruption, and lack of accountability. They are supposed to be the protectors of the public interest. The buck stops with them." I would go further: the buck stops with all board leaders. No one can rely on the efforts of others to get off the hook of knowing what is going on.

This book is divided into five sections and consists of nineteen brief, easily understandable chapters. Each chapter focuses on one particular aspect of the financial life of a nonprofit organization. Read the book from cover to cover or pick and choose topics as they impact the organization. A glossary at the end of the book can help with any terms that are not familiar and the appendix serves as a checklist of actions to take throughout the year.

Being a nonprofit leader, and especially a board member, is a big responsibility but it can be one that is both fun and personally rewarding. The ideas in this book should help make the task manageable and enjoyable. I hope the reader will conclude that finances can be accessible and useful to everyone in a nonprofit leadership position in helping him or her to participate in full and productive discussions of how best to fulfill the mission, goals, and priorities of our nonprofit organizations.

Allen J. Proctor
Worthington, Ohio
Fall 2010

Linking Mission to Money®
Finance for Nonprofit Leaders
Second Edition

❧ SECTION I ❧
PLANNING AND PRIORITIES

The greatest assets a board member can bring to a nonprofit are perspective, judgment, and common sense. Executives running nonprofits are consumed with overwhelming detail and the daily pressures of implementation. Board members, in contrast, have more limited involvement in the nonprofit and their day jobs will give them different perspectives on situations than the nonprofit encounters. Thus, when board members walk into the board room, they help most by pulling the discussion up to 40,000 feet where strategy is the main topic.

Finance should not discourage anyone from applying instinct and common sense to formulate a strategy to carry out the primary board duty, which is to make the nonprofit a reliable provider of a service that fulfills a useful need in the community. Even though it is the most important strategic goal of a nonprofit, it is often the goal most neglected amidst the pressures of running a nonprofit. Too many nonprofits fail to be reliable and sustainable service providers because they cut back during economic recessions when the community often needs their services the most. Achieving sustainability during recessions is a relentless challenge: there has not been a decade in this century or the last without at least one economic recession.

Surviving this recessionary trap requires strategic thinking and planning, which in turn require looking ahead. There are simple and complex tools to help nonprofits to look ahead, but the tool is less important than the effort. Sustainability requires being structurally balanced and developing the skill to know to set aside reserves when times are good so nonprofits can continue serving the community when times are bad.

I. BOARD FINANCIAL OVERSIGHT

Both new and veteran board members struggle to be helpful and engaged. Unfortunately, too many well-meaning board members never find the hook that makes their contributions seem valuable. That is even more common when it comes to finances. Nonprofits always seem to have too many things to do and too little cash with which to do them. Other than through personal donations, board members may feel that they have little to contribute toward understanding or solving this dilemma.

A board member's job can be summarized as two basic duties: to act with loyalty toward the nonprofit and to act with care. The following table provides brief notes to help keep these concepts at the front of mind in all dealings with nonprofits.

Loyalty means that the welfare of the organization comes before benefitting oneself or any individual, including the staff of the organization. No one should see the nonprofit as a means to benefit themselves or their business. All business transactions should be at competitive or concessionary prices.

Care means using common sense, asking tough questions, being businesslike and persistent, and exercising compromise when it is beneficial to the work of the nonprofit.

Finance should be viewed as merely another language that you can use in deciding which activities are most critical to fulfilling mission, how to carry them out, and how to pay for them in a way that makes the activities sufficiently sustainable that clients or patrons can rely on those activities year in and year out.

The most important financial issues need to be understood by all board members, but the key to understanding is not the level of detail. It is usually missing the forest that leads nonprofit boards astray, not missing the trees.

Duty of Loyalty:
- Independent
- Actions bring no personal gain
- Non-philanthropic transactions are arm's length

Duty of Care:
- Common sense; act as any prudent person would act
- Skepticism and diligence in asking basic and tough questions
- Discipline in establishing and following a regular process of oversight and review
- Resolve to insist that answers be understandable, convincing and thorough
- Judgment to know when and how to pursue an issue when others want to move on

---

As the items under duty of care suggest, common sense and judgment count as much as—and sometimes more than—expertise when it comes to fostering a successful and financially sustainable organization. Because common sense is so important, every member of the board has something to offer. The trick is to make sure that the treasure trove of common sense is routinely tapped.

The health of a nonprofit can be harmed by what is not discussed at the full board level, and it can be helped by spending the extra time to hear an individual board member's concerns. For instance, full board participation can be limited when a committee chair says, "I have looked over the numbers so let's save time by approving the budget without much discussion." The organization's ability to sustain a stable and reliable level of services may actually be enhanced by a board member who takes 20 minutes of an overly long board meeting trying to understand what a new program will cost and if it is affordable.

The most valuable step a board member can take to support, protect, and sustain the organization is to foster a culture that values diverse perspectives and encourages the communication of problems and concerns at all levels of the organization. One doesn't need to be a rocket scientist, or an accountant, to contribute to this discussion. The information a board needs can be provided without the complexity of financial statements and in a way that enhances the board's ability to focus on its important strategic issues without encroaching on the staff's operational issues.

This view of finance should benefit not just board members who may be intimidated by numbers but all board members who want help in focusing board deliberations on the critical issues of financial strategy and policy.

2. THE PRIMARY TASK IS TO SUSTAIN THE MISSION

The primary task of a nonprofit organization is to be a reliable provider of a service that fulfills a useful need in the community. Notice that I don't say that the organization's primary task is to grow or to do more than last year or even to be the best in the country. There are even nonprofits that are created for short-term purposes and that are intended to disappear in a year or two, but in this book I focus on nonprofits that are intended to exist for awhile.

A nonprofit is distinguished from a for-profit organization by having a primary mission to fulfill a community need that the market cannot or will not fulfill. This also means that the financial goal of a nonprofit is not to preserve itself as an organization but to preserve the ability to serve the mission. For example, a for-profit will change its products, its name, and its market as necessary to maintain the profitability of the business, particularly during an economic downturn. In contrast, the nonprofit will sustain serving its mission, regardless of financial difficulties, if the community still needs its services. This is summarized in the figure.

Community Need:
- 501(c)(3) status is granted by the IRS because you are filling a community need
- The nonprofit had to be created because the markets can't or won't provide the service
- The community has a vested interest in continuation of the needed non-profit service

Your duty is to ensure that your assigned mission will be fulfilled as long as the community has that need.

Sustainability:
- The ability to be there when you are most needed
- The need doesn't go away when the economy falters
- You may be most central to the vitality of your community when the chips are down.

The critical success factor of a nonprofit is to be a reliable provider of a service that fulfills a useful need in your community.

My emphasis on fulfillment of community need is based on the very existence of the notion of tax exemption, which allows people to deduct from their taxable income their charitable contributions to nonprofits. Most people refer to tax-exempt organizations as simply nonprofits. It is likely that the organization is a "501(c)(3)", which refers to the section of the Internal Revenue Code which grants an organization tax exempt status by the U.S. government. That status was granted *because* it is filling a community need. In fact, unless it is very small, every year organizations file a Form 990 with the IRS describing how their mission fulfills a community need and listing what they have done in the past year to fulfill that mission. If the IRS were to disagree that the activities continue to fulfill a community need, it has the ability to revoke an organization's tax exempt status.

As a leader of a nonprofit, one of the most basic duties is to ensure that the assigned mission will be fulfilled as long as the community has that need. I refer to this duty—the ability to be there when most needed—as *sustainability*. Throughout this book I will repeatedly argue that sustainability should form the foundation of every decision the board makes.

While this duty sounds obvious, it is actually difficult to execute and easy to forget amidst the myriad small decisions board leadership must continually confront. Many nonprofits lurch from crisis to crisis. They expand until economic recessions put them in financial crises that force them to cut back on services, often when the community need is the greatest. Whether a nonprofit in the arts, social services, healthcare, education, or another arena, the need for what it does doesn't go away when the economy falters. In fact, it is likely that a nonprofit's services are even more central to the vitality of the community when the chips are down.

Sustaining the mission of an organization is the primary task of nonprofit leadership. The primacy of sustainability forms the basis for how each leader should approach financial decisions. Steady, reliable, and predictable are the right words, but they run up against growth, expansion, and "meeting the need." When thinking about mission, always precede every major decision that has financial implications with the question: "How long can we sustain this change or ensure we will be able to provide this service?"

The dilemma of sustainability versus growth pervades the nonprofit world and one has to decide early on how the organization will deal with it. Is it better to provide a service and then suspend it when finances are tight? Or is it better to not provide the service at all? There is no clear-cut answer, nor is it always an either/or choice. Consider the following situations:

Suppose the organization provides temporary shelter for the homeless. Everyone believes strongly that there are not enough beds available in the community and that lives will be lost if there is not enough shelter, food, and healthcare for all comers. A site becomes available that would add

20 beds to the nonprofit's 200 bed system, and expand annual expenses by ten percent. Should the nonprofit acquire that site? Mission calls for it to expand. Sustainability requires one to first ask these questions:

- How would we change our operations to handle this expansion? Who on our staff would be affected and what is their view?

- How would we fund this added expense? If we plan to acquire additional governmental support, have we approached government officials and have they assured us of additional annual support for the foreseeable future?

- If we hope to receive additional foundation or United Way support, have we discussed our expansion with them and have they assured us of additional annual support for the foreseeable future?

- If we plan to increase private contributions, what actions will we take and what assurances should we expect before we go ahead with the acquisition?

The answers to these questions are critical to the ability to sustain this higher level of service but they are not likely to be uniformly positive or unambiguous. The government, foundations, or donors may not be able or willing to give unconditional assurances of expanded ongoing support. Without those assurances, the expansion of 20 beds may put at risk the current provision of 200 beds. The concept of sustainability next suggests that one ask these questions:

- Is one or two years of 220 beds worth the risk of budget strains forcing a cut back to 120 beds? What are the probabilities?

- Is the board prepared to increase its financial support by enough to prevent such a cut back scenario?

- Are there other nonprofits who are better able to acquire this site and sustain the expansion? If this nonprofit acquires this site is it precluding a stronger nonprofit from filling this shelter gap?

- If revenues don't materialize and one is forced to scale back, are there other nonprofits who would be able to make up for the lost beds or is the community dependent on this nonprofit for the 200 beds it currently provides?

These are the types of questions that sustainability requires one to consider each and every time one considers important organizational decisions.

Don't think that healthcare or indigent services are "special cases." Consider how sustainability can affect the decisions of a performing arts organization. The board wants to expand the performance season. It wants to ask its resident performers to remain under contract for a longer season, adjusting any other professional engagements accordingly. It will also need to ask part-time staff to shift more time to the organization. And, of course, more tickets will need to be sold and more donations solicited to make this effort successful.

- Can the organization reliably support a longer season financially?

- If it can't, can the staff and performers replace the lost income or have they foregone other options in order to block out more of their time for the longer season?

- Will donors be less supportive if the organization falls into financial difficulties than if it had not expanded at all?

These examples serve to remind us that sustaining a predictable and reliable level of services is a choice that nonprofit leaders must continually keep in mind when making decisions.

Be wary of expansion, especially when the economy is expanding. If a nonprofit grows and later cannot sustain its services, it may jeopardize its survival and undermine the constituents who relied upon it to sustain the expansion. Expansion should be approached cautiously with a clear, multiyear plan that gives one reasonable confidence that the nonprofit has taken the steps necessary for sustained success.

3. PLANNING: LINKING MISSION TO MONEY®

Finances play a major role in giving leaders confidence that the nonprofit can sustain its mission through thick and thin. But finances are not an end in themselves—they are simply the means to an end. Imagine the organization is an automobile and the leadership is the driver. Mission and community need represent the steering wheel, determining the path the organization will take. Finance—and all the jargon and budget-balancing hype it brings—represents the brake and accelerator pedals, determining how fast the organization travels along that path. The first focus should be the steering wheel; that is, how the nonprofit intends to meet the needs of the community.

Strategic planning is the tool most nonprofits use to "steer." Strategic plans are important and often many hours are spent in dedicated meetings putting together a good and coherent plan. These plans can create a tremendous forward-moving energy. Once completed though, it is a leader's responsibility to make sure the strategic plan does not sit on the shelf. Use the plan as a fundamental component of subsequent board meetings, budget deliberations, and performance reviews.

To ensure a strategic plan comes to fruition, link it with a financial plan. A useful financial plan should include a minimum of three years: the current year, the year for which one is making decisions (ideally as part of the budget process), and the following year. Additional years can be valuable for planning fundraising or physical expansions. Remember, the major value of a financial plan is to show the implications of decisions, so don't hesitate to use a financial plan to prompt good "what if" discussions of alternative ways to fulfill mission.

The financial plan links mission with the reality of the resources available. To create this link, one needs to be familiar with two tools of any sustainable financial plan: models and structural balance.

Forecasting and Models

The strength of a financial plan is that it lets one look into the future. That means one must *forecast.* The word forecast may needlessly put fear into many board and staff members' minds because pundits love to point out how often forecasts are wrong: from weather forecasts and national economic forecasts to federal budget forecasts and company earnings forecasts.

While it would be very helpful to know what the future will bring, the principal value of forecasting models has never been to predict the future but rather to use models to see how some actions depend on other actions so the user of the model can see the big picture emerge from many details. With that greater perspective, it then becomes easier to make better decisions. Some wariness about forecasting may also arise because of misconceptions about what constitutes a model and how it works.

Financial planning and forecasting do not require lots of training or staff. In a small organization, board members may need to do some of this planning and forecasting. In a larger organization, the staff will probably do this work but board members should still know enough about the purpose of planning and forecasting to be able to join in deliberations.

Whether they are simple and small or complex and enormous, what good models all have in common is a consistent way of viewing how something works. A model most often is a set of equations in a spreadsheet that ties staff and salaries to payroll and benefits, number of guests to prices and earned revenue, fundraising to specific programs and uses, and total revenues and expenses to resources and obligations, and so on. It also ties each year to the year before and to the years after.

I began my professional career constructing models and I have been a user of models for more than 30 years. The skill in building a model is to ensure consistency between the parts and the whole: the parts add up to a whole that is internally consistent and that faithfully represents a legitimate view of the way the world works.

Good decision-making requires consistent thinking. Forecasting with the help of models allows one to evaluate how consistent one's thinking is. This test for consistency far outweighs the details of how large, complex, or simplistic is the model. Do not make the mistake of assuming that complexity necessarily provides better consistency. In many cases the opposite is true: it is much more difficult to ensure the consistency of viewpoint of a large or complex model than the consistency of a simple model.

Use models to test your thinking:

- Is the underlying view of the world or the organization represented by the model still valid?

- What are the implications of one decision versus another?

- Which action has a greater impact, option one or option two?

- What outcome are we aiming for and what types of actions are likely to help us achieve that outcome?

- Can we identify which actions are more likely and which ones less likely to achieve our goals?

- Which actions may take the longest to reach our goals? The fastest?

Again, consistent simplicity in plans and forecasts is vastly better than inconsistent complexity. Here's an example of a simplistic forecast that can be valuable to deliberations: Consider a forecasting approach that simply assumes 3% annual growth in expenses. One may scoff at 3%, saying "that's just an arbitrary number." Would one feel better if we got to 3% through a large number of complex and hard-to-understand mathematical equations? Why? Will the organization succeed or fail based on whether the 3% turns out to be actual future expense growth? Hardly.

But the wisdom of decisions may likely depend on understanding the implications of 3% growth. Why? Because the forecast allows one to see the implications of 3% expense growth. For example, one can test its implications by seeing how 5% expense growth, or 1% expense growth, would advance or limit achievement of the nonprofit's goals and objectives. How one determined to use 3% in planning is less important than how one evaluated the implications of 3% on the plans.

Larger organizations should consider more sophisticated ways to use a model to link their forecast to economic, political, and demographic information about the demand for the organization's services and the sources of the organization's revenues. Nevertheless, this should be done only if the complexity doesn't interfere with the ability to see and understand the implications of decisions and choices.

Structural Balance

The greatest value of a model is its use as the underpinning of a multi-year financial plan that allows one to evaluate the likelihood of implementing and sustaining the strategic plan. Structural balance meshes the concepts of budget balance and sustainability with the tools of financial planning and forecasting. In doing so, structural balance becomes a powerful concept for providing sustainability and stability to an organization.

The majority of nonprofits are charged with providing services that citizens demand or need, year in and year out. The job of a nonprofit is to get as close to being a reliable provider of those services as it possibly can. The most essential, fundamental, and long-lasting solution to this challenge is to bring a nonprofit's finances into what we call structural balance. The term "structural balance" implies that the "structure" of a nonprofit's finances is such that a "balance" is achieved between the services that are provided and the local community's and economy's ability to pay for these services over a prolonged period of time such as a business cycle. The figure below illustrates this concept.

Illustration of Structural Balance and Imbalance

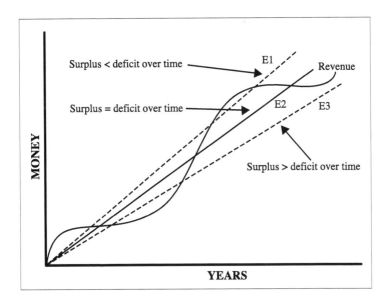

If one had revenue sources that changed over time as shown in this figure, which growth path of expenditures would be preferable? Path E1 shows chronic deficits amidst brief periods of surplus, caused by an unsustainable level of expenditures. Only during the relatively short period of time when revenues are growing strongly can these expenditures be supported by revenues. The organization with this revenue and expenditure structure will be continually cutting back on services and overextending its staff and its resources.

Path E3 shows chronic surpluses and brief deficits arising from providing a minimal level of expenditures and services. More services are possible at all times except during the depths of the revenue decline. The organization with this revenue and expense structure is chronically receiving more revenues than it needs to sustain its current level of services. This organization is underfulfilling its mission because it could sustain a higher level of services than it currently does.

Path E2 shows that surpluses balance deficits over time and this set of expenses can be supported by existing revenue sources over time. Some periods have surpluses and some have deficits, but the amount of surpluses is enough to support the deficits if the organization can set aside and save the surpluses until the deficits emerge. In Chapter 16 I will discuss tools the board has available to set aside and save its surpluses when it has achieved structural balance.

Ideally a nonprofit will be in structural balance and the sustainability of its mission will be secure. To know if this is true the staff should construct a financial plan that reflects their beliefs about the components of the organization's revenue and expense structures. Then use the plan to answer the following questions, which should help develop a feel for how stable this structure is likely to be over the course of various possible future events.

- Assume the local economy races ahead: which revenues will grow faster and which ones are likely to be unaffected; which expenditures will grow or decline and which are likely to be unaffected? Will the need for your services diminish if the local economy surges ahead?

- How about a sharp decline in the local economy? Which of your revenue sources will suffer and which will hold their own? How about the organization's expenditures? Will demand for its services increase or decrease during an economic decline?

- Which expenditures can it control and which are independent?

- What are the implications of these scenarios on budget balance? If surpluses are likely, will the organization set aside reserves or expand its programs? If so, how?

- If deficits are likely, does the organization have reserves to call upon? For how long? Are there some revenues it can increase? Expenditures it can decrease?

- Can the organization sustain its current service levels? For how long? How long does it want to or need to sustain those levels?

- Which expenses or services would it be able or willing to cut back immediately?

- What do these scenarios imply about the organization's ability to achieve its strategic plan and fulfill its mission? What would it need to do differently now in order to achieve its strategic plan despite a decline in the local economy? Will improvement in the local economy help it achieve its strategic plan?

This question and answer process will provide a better understanding of the meaning of structural balance and of its value to the organization and the community.

Structural balance is not permanent because revenues and expenditures fluctuate due to influences that are beyond a nonprofit's direct control. A financial planning process that contains structural balance as one of its objectives will continually evaluate whether evolving expenditures, revenues, policy decisions, and priorities remain compatible. Priorities must be constantly reviewed as the needs of the nonprofit and its community change. In other words, can expenditures needed by the community continue to be sustained by revenues or must further changes occur?

Key Questions about Planning and Priorities

1. Do all board members fulfill their duty of care by asking questions, revealing their views, and participating in discussions?

2. Do you know how your revenues and expenses respond to the business cycle?

3. Do you have a financial plan that describes your strategy and how you expect it to be reflected in your services, expenses, fundraising, and earned revenues over the next three to five years?

4. Is your organization a reliable provider of a useful need of the community?

⦿ SECTION II ⦾
BUILDING A MISSION-FOCUSED BUDGET

The budget is the first implementation step of a multi-year plan. A good budget links the mission to how money is spent and to the evolving needs of the community. Throughout the course of the year, nonprofit leaders must understand that a budget is a story which happens to have numbers associated with it. It is a story that tells where the nonprofit wants to go and why, what it takes to get there, and what the nonprofit is doing this year in order to move ahead on that path. Many approaches can help assemble a budget that does this. Focus less on the approach and more on the purpose – the story—of the budget. And tell that story as often as possible: to staff, donors, funders, and the community.

We are often misled by our use of the term "nonprofit." It is a misnomer. Nonprofits need profits in order to survive, no differently than any business. How to use those profits is what distinguishes nonprofits from for-profits. Unfortunately too many nonprofit leaders ignore this need for profitability by allowing a nonprofit to be unprofitable over time (a structural deficit).

Wise nonprofits are profitable and use those profits to build reserves to improve and maintain services, to try innovative approaches, and to sustain services through recession and crisis. And sustaining and stabilizing services through those difficult times will almost always call for using those reserves to finance an operating deficit. Too many nonprofit leaders are not mindful of this need for stabilizing service and instead insist that a nonprofit balance its budget during a recession or other financial crisis.

At the same time, the search for sustainability is rarely advanced by playing it safe or being "conservative" in approaching budgets. Well-intended efforts to be conservative can often lead to unintended consequences that actually increase risk and the nonprofit's vulnerability to recession. Always test any "conservative" proposal for how it will impact the nonprofit's ability to serve the community's needs today and through economic recession and recovery.

4. BUDGETING: IMPLEMENTING A NONPROFIT'S PLAN AND MISSION

Perhaps at the last board meeting, the executive director announced that the time to build the next year's budget was approaching. Board and staff envision a process of endless meetings, endless detail, thousands of yes/no decisions, and tables that glaze the eyes. That, unfortunately, is an accurate description of too many nonprofits' budget building processes and I also roll my eyes when I see it. While there is certainly a technical aspect to preparing a budget, that aspect and the accompanying fine level of detail have no place in a board meeting or even a board finance committee meeting. If numbers and dollars seem intimidating, be reminded that the budget is really quite simple in purpose and content: it is *a plan of action*, and it is just using dollars as the language to help board leaders sort through priorities and capabilities.

The board's role is to *oversee* budget preparation, not to prepare the budget. In Chapter 9 I will provide some sample instructions and forms for staff to use in constructing a budget that can be more easily evaluated, approved, and monitored over the year.

My main goal in this chapter is to argue convincingly that the most important role leadership can play in the budget preparation process is to insist that the budget be firmly grounded in the strategic vision and financial plan agreed to by the board and the staff when they addressed the questions posed in Chapter 3. Firm grounding means that the budget has specific goals and objectives to advance the strategic plan, and that each goal and objective has specific progress milestones that can be reviewed at every board meeting.

27

Too many budget processes are short-sighted, one-year-at-a-time exercises to balance revenues and expenditures. In periods of fiscal stress or economic uncertainty, a budget process with a one-year horizon makes it easy to postpone difficult strategic decisions in the hope that things will get better in the next year or so. It is important to resist this.

The primary goal of the budget should be to make it the first implementation step of the multi-year financial plan. This approach will force the budget decision-making process beyond the limits of a short-term, largely budget-balancing exercise while at the same time providing board and the staff with an objective and tangible way to conduct budget deliberations in the broader context of community need and service sustainability.

This budget-within-a-plan approach is the best mechanism available to evaluate the impact of current-year budget decisions and the organization's long-term ability to sustain the its mission. By insisting that the budget be prepared to represent the "first year" of the financial plan, budget decisions will routinely be placed in the context of long-term strategy and mission, which are the only budget issues in which a board should directly engage. In contrast, when the current-year budget is the only data to review, the board's role in budget preparation is unnecessarily forced into non-strategic or technical areas that are best left to the staff.

In the 1990s, a thoughtful model for this strategic approach to budgeting was formulated for the government sector and there is much that the nonprofit sector can borrow from that model. Forward-thinking local governments concluded that their budget processes needed to be more responsive to local priorities and that they needed to make sure their budget decisions were moving their governments in the direction their citizens wanted to go. I was fortunate to be a founding member of that effort. We concluded that the conventional approaches to budgeting weren't even satisfying to our own elected officials, who often felt themselves to be less participants than observers in budgetary decision-making. I think many nonprofit board members would echo those same sentiments about feeling detached from their own budget process.

These conclusions were reached by the National Advisory Council on State and Local Budgeting when it completed its work with the publication in 1998 of *Recommended Budget Practices: A Framework for Improved State and Local Government Budgeting.* This group represented an unprecedented cooperative effort by organizations with widely diverse interests to examine and agree on key aspects of good budgeting. The Council membership spanned academia, labor unions, the public finance industry, and eight organizations representing elected officials, government administrators, and finance professionals at both the state and local levels. Over several years of deliberations, it converged on a goal-driven approach to budgeting that uses a long-range perspective to integrate the many dimensions of budgeting, including political, managerial, planning, communication, and financial.

The Council's framework for thinking about budgeting can be useful for many nonprofit boards. It states that the fundamental purpose of the budget process is to "help decision-makers make informed decisions about the provision of services." I think this observation is simple yet profound: This council with enormously diverse interests agreed that the purpose of the budget process should be to help the nonprofit leader to be *informed* well enough to make good *decisions.* There is nothing passive about that sentence. And it should be the minimum expectation of what the budget process should be for every leader in a nonprofit:

You will be informed well enough about the budget proposals that you can make good decisions about how best to achieve your priorities with the resources available.

Accept no less from the budget.

5. REVIEWING PRIORITIES

About one quarter into the new fiscal year the board should reconvene for a reality check on vision and priorities. The outcome of this meeting should be the list of priorities and outcomes for the staff to use in formulating the budget for next year. This meeting will ensure that vision and priorities will be an integral part of governance rather than stale concepts that are put in a binder and left on a shelf to gather dust.

Three Crucial Questions

There are three questions that it is crucial the board ask itself before the staff begins preparing the next fiscal year's budget. These are fundamental issues that don't easily fit into a routine board agenda.

First, ask whether spending reflects priorities. Start with the facts: confirm that spending last year was consistent with mission and last year's priorities. After that, do the same for the budget just started: Is the current budget consistent with the current priorities? Be especially wary of responses like "that is how we have always spent our money." Times change, needs change, priorities change; spending should be changing too. As a quick check on mission focus, look at the percentages of expenses spent on programming, fundraising, and administration and how those percentages have changed over the past five or so years. If the share devoted to programming is trending downward, it is time to refocus on priorities. Also, try matching revenues for a particular program with its expenses. Is the program self-supporting? Should it be? Is the value of the program commensurate with the net cost to the organization?

Second, ask how well the organization sticks to its plans and priorities. Take a look at how the last year ended compared with the budget approved for last year. Was spending growth where expected? Revenue growth too? Did the final audit confirm what the last budget report said as the year ended? If the answer was "no" to any of these questions, review the oversight process because plans and reviews aren't consistent with what is happening.

Third, ask what events might compel the organization to deviate from delivering on priorities in the current year and the year which will soon be budgeted. Be pessimistic—a problem anticipated is easier to resolve than a crisis.

At the conclusion of this review the board should be convinced that spending is indeed consistent with priorities. It should also be convinced that the organization can realistically continue with these priorities over the coming year or so.

Making Changes

After the board has answered those three crucial questions, it now needs to decide where to change or tweak those priorities for the coming year, if at all. With those priorities in hand, turn them over to the staff and ask them to begin preparing estimates of the resources they believe will be necessary for the next year to meet those priorities. Over the next few months they will review progress in the current year, and develop proposals and cost and resource estimates for the coming year consistent with those strategic priorities.

When the board receives the staff's proposed budget, it first should look to see if the bottom line is consistent with the strategic plan and where the organization is in the business cycle. Does it reflect the priorities given to the staff earlier? If the budget proposal does not have the bottom line or priorities approved earlier in the year, the board is obligated to revise its priorities, not to nitpick the estimates of revenues or expenses.

Remember, the board's role is to set priorities and to oversee the accomplishment of those priorities within the overall availability of resources. Board members need to resist dwelling on the estimates for any particular area. The executive director, and if the organization is small, perhaps the treasurer too, has the role of making sure the estimates are good and well-supported before the budget is presented to the board. In a large board, the finance committee may handle the first few rounds of budget review with the staff before a final recommendation is passed to the full board.

It is not appropriate for the board to change spending without also changing the priorities and expectations for service delivery. Don't be the board that cuts spending but tells the staff that they must still provide the same service levels as before. If they can do the same with less, then the board has already failed because it hasn't been doing its annual reality checks very well in trying to provide the best services with the resources available!

Take a look at the timeline for the budget process on the following page. Notice that the process starts nine months or more before the start of the next fiscal year. Once one thinks of the budget as the result of a goal-setting and priority-setting process, one will begin to see the budget process as a continual, year-round process of high level discussions about vision, goals, and priorities, with an ongoing set of reality checks.

A Timetable for Building and Monitoring a Budget

	July 1 Fiscal Year	January 1 Fiscal Year
Readjust current budget to be consistent with audited results of year just completed	September before budget year	March before budget year
Board reviews long-term goals, vision, and priorities for next year	October	April
Staff does first re-estimate of current budget and project next year revenues	November	May
Staff begins to formulate proposed budget linking it to broad goals	December	June
Staff prioritizes proposals, re-estimating current year's budget, and projecting next year's revenues	February	August
Staff makes proposals to the Board to meet its priorities and outcomes within projected revenues (for larger organizations, this proposal may be made to the Finance Committee)	March	September
Staff revises proposals and presents to Board (for larger organizations this may be presented to the Executive committee)	April	October
Budget revised and final version presented to full board for approval	May	November
Budget published and distributed to staff and interested parties	June	December
	Budget Year Starts	**Budget Year Starts**

Review audit of year just completed and validate feasibility of new budget	September	March
Review achievement of first quarter goals and priorities and validate feasibility of the year's timetable, goals, and resource adequacy	October	April
Review achievement of second quarter goals	January	July
Review achievement of third quarter goals ...	April	October
	Budget Year Ends	**Budget Year Ends**
Review audit of completed year	October	March
Review and file IRS Form 990	February	July

6. FIVE FEATURES OF AN EFFECTIVE BUDGET

The prior chapter talked about ways for the board to review and adapt its goals and priorities. Based on the guidance that came from that review, a budget for the coming year will be prepared. Once the board has received the proposed budget—replete with numbers and, hopefully, graphs and text—it is time to make sure that the budget facilitates the organization's ability to meet and sustain its mission. This budget should include all that is necessary for the organization to achieve its mission, as well as take a solid step forward along its long-term plan. This chapter assumes that the budget preparation process was started properly by incorporating board dialogue about what the organization is all about, what it needs to accomplish over the next several years, and what it can realistically achieve over the next 12 months.

The previously mentioned National Advisory Council on State and Local Budgeting came up with a definition of the characteristics of an effective budgeting process:

"...the budget process is not simply an exercise in balancing revenues and expenditures one year at a time, but is strategic in nature, encompassing a multi-year financial and operating plan that allocates resources on the basis of identified goals. A good budget process moves beyond the traditional concept of line item expenditure control, providing [motivation] and flexibility to staff that can lead to improved program efficiency and effectiveness."

Therefore, from the board perspective, the hallmark of an effective budget is that it enables board members to be actively engaged in advancing the mission of the organization. That engagement occurs when the budget incorporates the following five features identified by the National Advisory Council:

1. Long-term perspective

2. Linkages to broad organizational goals

3. Focus on results and outcomes

4. Effective communication to stakeholders

5. Constructive motivation of staff

If the board has not yet formulated a vision, articulated mission, or developed a strategic plan, the organization is behind the curve in providing staff with the necessary context for them to be able to produce a budget that has these characteristics.

Long-Term Perspective

A budget should be approached as the first step into the future of the organization. Each budget decision will have a consequence on future years and budget discussions should be focused heavily on the desirability and relative importance of those consequences. The budget should clearly and explicitly address the following questions. The duty of the board is to make certain that the answers are consistent with the organization's mission and long-term plan.

- Is service demand likely to grow in future years? If so, does the budget start planning for that growth?

- Will current grant and philanthropic efforts be adequate to support such growth? What does the proposed budget do to sustain those efforts? Will the level of service delivery and/or financial condition fostered by this budget encourage donors and grantors to meet the level of gifts anticipated in the budget and plan?

- Will any facilities need significant repair or modification in the next few years? If so, does the organization expect to perform those repairs? How will it pay for them if it does and what are the consequences if it doesn't?

- Will some savings be used now or in the near future? If so, is there a plan of action to have sufficient savings set aside in time?

- Does the organization anticipate borrowing now or in the near future? If so, is it fostering good banking relationships and getting its balance sheet into a lender-appealing shape?

Even if the organization plans to maintain the status quo, it should have a clear understanding of what the status quo means and how it will perform and be perceived several years from now if it remains essentially unchanged.

- How might the environment change in the next few years? More or fewer clients or patrons? A different client or patron profile?

- Will it be easier or more difficult to obtain government and corporate support?

- Are donors likely to be able to sustain or increase giving?

- Will other nonprofits be undertaking major fundraising campaigns that may draw on the same donor pool?

- Will costs grow over the next few years? Can the fee structure support that growth? Do other revenue sources also need to grow?

Hopefully, these questions make it clear that even maintaining the status quo requires the budget process to look ahead.

Linkages to Broad Organizational Goals

In a planning meeting at the beginning of the budget process the board should have formulated some goals. With the proposed budget now in hand, make sure that at least one action is being taken in the next year to address each goal. Linking the budget to specific actions is important if goals are to be achieved because the budget process is where the rubber of resources meets the road of vision.

Making sure that goals are being addressed doesn't necessarily mean big projects requiring lots of money. Meeting goals is more often a decision to refocus existing resources on the highest priorities than it is a decision to seek new funds to address new activities. I have overseen many budgets in which resources were refocused or reallocated across activities to address a new set of goals from the past year. The new set of goals did not call for increased spending. The significance of making sure the proposed budget addresses each goal is that it requires the staff to demonstrate or reaffirm to *itself* that activities and resources are indeed linked to the main goals of the organization.

Consider a social service organization with one of its goals to expand its presence in an emerging immigrant community. A no-cost link to this goal could be a commitment to establish relationships with several leaders in that community over the next year. A low-cost link could be to hire one additional staff for outreach to that community. A higher cost link could be to build or rent a satellite facility in that community. The important thing is not that there is a dollar figure linked to each goal but that there is an activity or special effort linked to each goal each year.

Consider an arts organization with one of its goals to develop audience in the under-40 population, but there are no additional monies available this year to advance this goal. During the budget process, consider ways to redirect the current level of effort to make inroads into that population. How about the board nominating committee: how can their activities for the coming year foster connection with this new audience through board recruiting?

Focus on Results and Outcomes

Why spend money unless one expects something in return? While this question seems obvious, I would guess that too many board members have approved their share of budgets without placing any explicit expectations on themselves or on the staff of what results or outcomes they expect to see one year later. Board approval of a spending plan doesn't provide much value to an organization if all the board has done is to box itself into the uninteresting decision-making corner of saying either "spend more here" or "spend less there."

On the other hand, board approval of what the organization is expected to accomplish over the next year along with board approval of an objective measure of that accomplishment does provide enormous leadership and guidance to the organization.

A budget is a plan of action that happens to use dollars as a means of sorting through priorities and capabilities. Budget balance is the simplest part of the exercise. Yet many boards spend all their time on the balancing effort and relatively little time discussing what the organization can and should accomplish in order to ensure the organization's value to the community.

The most certain way for a board member to remain in touch with the essence of what the organization does is to use the budget process to document exactly what another year of the organization's existence should accomplish. Moreover, when that year is over, if it can measure and document that it did what it said it would do, it will likely have huge benefits in attracting donors and grantors. Through this process the board members also will have more confidence that the time and money they personally are committing to this organization are making a difference.

Effective Communication to Stakeholders

The biblical notion that a lighted candle should not be put under a bushel applies to the budget process as well. I am constantly amazed at the invisibility of so many nonprofits' budgets. What a lost opportunity to communicate vision, mission, and a focused plan of action. If the organization uses the budget to challenge itself to make a difference in an objective and verifiable way, it should want to broadcast that.

View the budget as an opportunity to communicate what the organization is about and why money devoted to the organization is money well spent. Donors favor organizations that are confident enough about their value to the community to subject themselves to measurement and verification. And a promise whose achievement is measured is always good material for a press release and a news story.

Such an explicit commitment to mission is also worth communicating to staff, especially in a larger organization where the activities of the board and executive director are not as visible to the staff. A budget that shows the staff that the organization spends money consistent with its priorities will contribute to good morale, and it is a much better way to communicate than water cooler speculation.

Many organizations remain fearful of having how they raise and spend money easily available and understood beyond the executive director and board. If the organization doesn't have a budget summary of its major intentions for the coming year that is made readily available to staff, donors, clients and/or patrons, ask why. Could it be because the board doesn't have a clear idea of what is supposed to be accomplished in the coming year? If that is the case, the board isn't doing its job to set priorities and formulate a coherent strategic direction. If it is doing its job, why make it a secret?

There is no more effective way to communicate priorities and demonstrate commitment to those priorities than through the budget, which shows the organization has put its money where its mouth is.

Constructive Motivation of Staff

While there are many technical ways to use a budget to foster good operational management by staff, I want to emphasize the notion of using the board's role in overseeing the budget process to energize staff by giving them ownership and excitement in the allocation of resources. Since the board oversees the budget but doesn't prepare it, one may wonder how the board can do this.

The answer is simple: the rules of the game determine how the game is played. For example, many budgets have a rule that says "use it or lose it." In other words, any part of the budget that doesn't use all the funds it was allocated will have the next year's budget reduced to the level it actually used in the past year. This is a great incentive to spend as much money by the end of the year in order to "protect" one's resources. A rule like this has encouraged spending on low priority areas and it has discouraged any incentive for staff to suggest reallocation of resources since giving up budget funds provides no guarantee of getting them back.

Alternatively, suppose the board gives a good performance review to the executive director if he spends under budget and perhaps a negative one if he goes over budget. What the board really wants is for the executive director to achieve the organization's priorities and goals. Budget balance is a limitation and a constraint. Staying within the constraint without achieving goals is not good performance. But if coming in under budget is the yardstick applied to the executive director, it probably also sends a message to staff to value spending restraint over goal achievement.

What the board needs is a budget process that encourages ideas from staff and that fosters dialogue across the organization about how to make the most progress in its goals from the resources available. To do this, one doesn't want a process that encourages turf wars or that encourages "hiding money" within the budget to protect certain areas from board or executive director scrutiny.

There are many budget approaches that can motivate staff and I will describe one approach in Chapter 9. The main point here is simply that, if the board has agreed on the strategic goals of the organization, the budget process can be used to create excitement among the staff to formulate ways to advance those goals. The board will find the process more satisfying, and the staff will find energy in their participation.

7. WHEN IS A BUDGET "CONSERVATIVE"?

The most misused phrase in finance is *conservative budgeting*. It has no agreed upon definition and one must be wary lest its use serve the personal biases of the speaker, often to justify arbitrary revenue or expense decisions. Nonprofit leaders charged with setting the strategic direction of the organization should focus on the "conserve" part of the word "conservative" to ensure a budget that gives the best chance of conserving or sustaining priorities and adhering to mission through the up's and down's of the economy.

There are good ways to be conservative and counterproductive ways to be conservative. To be appropriately "conserve-ative," it is critical that the approach to the budget is "do no harm," in the sense that the approach should lay the best foundation under current circumstances for continued adherence to mission and priorities for the following years. Remember, the primary duty of a nonprofit is to be a stable, reliable provider of a community need regardless of the economy. *The value of thinking ahead and using a multi-year financial plan to do this effectively cannot be overemphasized.*

A good conservative practice is to ensure that service levels do not exceed the level that is sustainable over the business cycle. The chart below illustrates an expenditure level that is sustainable because the size of deficits during economic recession are balanced by surpluses during economic recovery. To be "conserve-ative," services should not be expanded beyond that level.

Sustain Services Over the Business Cycle

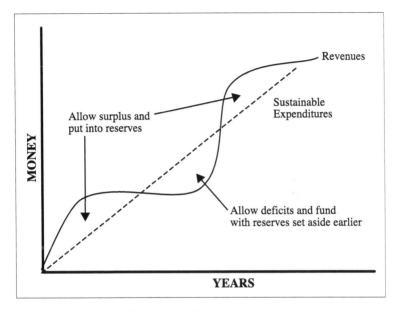

A second good conservative practice is to demand that budgets be in surplus during strong economic times and to make sure that those surpluses are set aside in board-designated reserves for use when the economy tumbles or some other financial crisis occurs.

In contrast, it is unwise and inappropriate to try to be conservative by hiding expected surpluses, by lowballing revenues in order to "build a cushion" in secret. When the year ends the surplus will be apparent to everyone, but that practice will have undermined credibility later when times are truly tough and donors, clients, and staff will disregard any statement that the nonprofit is short on funds.

Demanding that budgets be balanced during economic recession is the antithesis of conserving mission. Reserves should be used during recession or crisis to finance deficits in order to maintain mission services. Recessions are not the time to maintain strong balance sheets. Rather, strong balance sheets are built during economic recoveries precisely so that those resources can be spent down to maintain a reliable level of services to the community.

It is particularly inappropriate for the board to "position" itself with regard to biasing revenue or spending estimates in order to manipulate expected surpluses or deficits. It is not the board's role to be involved in this aspect of budgeting. The necessary level of expertise to produce quality estimates lies with staff. Good leaders will insist that the staff provide their best estimates of the most likely outcomes and that they not try to second guess what the leadership would like to hear. If there are concerns that the organization may be approaching some adverse events such as an economic downturn, it is more appropriate to leave the staff estimates alone and to decide to spend less than 100 percent of estimated revenues, budget a surplus, and put the "extra" revenue into reserves.

It is also inappropriate to hold down spending on mission priorities in order to enlarge surpluses or reduce deficits in order to demonstrate that the organization is "lean and mean" or "efficient". Mission is what nonprofits are all about. Being "conservative" by denying high-priority spending in order to build a larger financial cushion is contrary to conserving mission. Similarly, when the economy is weak and deficits appear, spending reductions should not come from key mission programming, and spending certainly should not be cut in order to avoid using reserves.

Being truly efficient and effective requires investing in infrastructure, overhead, and administration. Unfortunately, many nonprofits think they are being conservative by having poor facilities, outdated computer systems, and inadequate staff. This "pride in being tattered" is intended to impress donors that their contributions are being wisely used and

"100% going to programs." This is unwise and counterproductive. Nonprofit staff need good working conditions no less than do for-profit workers. Underspending on overhead and support systems can actually undermine the long-term effectiveness of programs.

Donors' notions of conservative can also be harmful to the financial well-being of the nonprofit. It is too common for donors to place restrictions that their gifts cannot be spent on overhead and can be spent only for specific programs. The donor believes that the restriction ensures the nonprofit will spend wisely and on mission priorities. Unfortunately, more often these restrictions serve to steer nonprofit spending away from the nonprofit's mission priorities and toward the donor's personal priorities. They certainly limit the nonprofit's financial flexibility to respond to changing circumstances.

Good conservative approaches react to immediate issues in a way that enhances the organization's ability to sustain its mission in future years. For example, if extra money becomes available, first decide if the funds are certain to recur or not. If one can't yet be sure that the funds will recur, don't spend it on items that will require additional or continued spending in future budgets; spend it on one-time expenses such as equipment or else put it into reserves or pay off some debt.

On the other hand, if money is suddenly short, conserving mission argues that nonprofits should try to focus any expense reductions on secondary areas, such as purchases that can easily be postponed a year or discretionary spending that is not essential to mission or priorities. Those decisions are best made in advance because good ideas may need some research or investigation. In the press of the moment people most likely cut back on the activities foremost in their minds, which are likely to be the higher priorities.

Revenue and Expenditure Estimates

I've just said not to let personal notions of "conservative finance" influence the board's role in budget preparation, and I have also said that boards should not get involved in tinkering with the staff's revenue and expense estimates. I would be remiss if I left the impression that the budget and its estimates are none of the board's business. That is not the case; what is the board's business is making sure that the estimates are tied to priorities and strategy in a way that everyone can understand so that the board's decisions can *conserve* mission and priorities throughout the year and into the future.

For example, nonprofit leaders should insist that spending estimates be clearly tied to levels of effort and provision of specific service levels. The staff should be convincing that they will execute at a level consistent with the board's mandated mission and priorities and on a timeline that the board finds acceptable and is able to monitor effectively over the course of the year.

Think of a spending estimate as a project with the following:

- a resource requirement,

- a set of milestones, and

- a set of measurable objectives and outcomes.

The duty of a board member is to be convinced that these three blanks are adequately filled in for the significant components of the expense budget (that's the reality check) and that the overall picture is consistent with the consensus on mission and priorities.

The duty with respect to revenue estimates is quite different. Revenue estimates are forecasts of the future, so it is very likely they could be wrong. There is no such thing as an "accurate" forecast. The key questions for the board to address are:

- What sequence of events is assumed to occur that will result in the revenues being received in the amount and at the time estimated?

- When will the board review whether the anticipated sequence of events has occurred?

- What steps will be taken if the actual revenue turns out to be significantly higher or lower than expected?

Remember that a revenue forecast is based on a prediction that a certain sequence of events or a specific scenario will occur. Keep in mind that there are always many possible scenarios, and that the staff's revenue estimate implicitly assumes a particular scenario.

For example, consider a museum's forecast for revenue from admission fees for the coming year. Admission revenue forecasts have key assumptions about significant seasons, such as school vacation weeks or the Christmas holidays. The staff should be able to say, "We expect increased attendance to 5,000 with revenue of $25,000 over the holidays. If attendance instead remains at last year's lower levels we will know by January 1 and will reduce our revenue estimate by $5,000."

Alternatively, the estimate for fundraising will include some assumptions regarding key donors: "We anticipate the Widget Corporation will renew its pledge for $10,000 in October. If we don't have the pledge in hand by November 30, we will reduce our revenue estimate by $10,000."

These stories or scenarios are the board's tool to monitor the "reality" of the revenue estimates. If the staff did not provide a series of scenarios, press them to do so. Staff stories should have specific milestones or drop-dead dates so there will be reliable ways to know when the organization is ahead or behind in the budget.

When considering proposed expenditures based on anticipated fundraising, it is good conservative practice to require a certain level of cash and written pledges be in hand before authorizing the expenditure in order to reduce the potential loss if fundraising falls short. It is especially valuable to delay disbursements until at least some pledges have been paid. To do otherwise is essentially allowing your nonprofit to be the "banker" to the donor by advancing the funds before the donor has paid. It is also a reality that some pledges, and particularly pledges solicited by telephone, will not be fully paid.

When asked for a gift pledge, rarely will a donor give a clear "no." Instead they often agree to consider it and think about a pledge. And hope can spring eternal for the development staff to obtain payment for that pledge – until the last day of the fiscal year when they must admit that the budgeted revenue will not materialize. At this point the expenditures have occurred, the budget has a shortfall, and the organization's ability to reconsider the expenditure has become non-existent. Shaving the pledge estimate by a percentage based on recent collection experience is appropriately conservative.

Despite the difficulties inherent in fundraising, good conservative practice requires that the expectation for pledges be set against a reasonable timetable, which, if not met, should warrant reducing budgeted fundraising revenues. Reducing a fundraising revenue estimate does not mean giving up on the donor; rather, it means that the organization is turning its reliance to what is real (the gift has not yet been received) and adjusting its plans while it can still do so in an orderly manner that preserves its mission and priorities.

8. PROFIT-MAKING BY NONPROFITS

I t is curious that charitable organizations are called non-profits because it is a misconception that nonprofits are supposed to lose money. On the contrary, all nonprofits need profits in order to survive.

Nonprofits are characterized by <u>how</u> they spend their profits, not by <u>whether</u> they earn profits. The principles that govern nonprofits mandate that nonprofits plow their profits back into the level, quality, or reliability of services. Sustainability requires that the organization have some money set aside to weather bad years. The only way to get that money is to earn more than it spends in some years; that is a profit. Endowments are accumulated by setting aside extra donations; once again, a profit. Deficits are financed with reserve funds, and reserves are past profits.

Similarly, most nonprofits provide a number of services. A user's ability to pay often varies with the service. The reality is that a viable nonprofit makes ends meet by offering some services that do not fully pay for themselves (unprofitable services) and other services that bring in more money than they cost (profitable services). While a for-profit may have some items that it sells at a loss (loss-leaders), the role of those items is to attract customers who will simultaneously purchase profitable items so that the total purchases of each customer are profitable.

In contrast, the nonprofit is willing to have all the services it provides to some client/customers be unprofitable. To be viable, however, the nonprofit must be able to attract some profitable client/customers as well. The link between mission relevance and profitability is a critical strategic policy, illustrated in the Linking Mission to Money® grid below.

We will use this chart extensively in Chapter 12, *Financial Reports: Linking Mission to Money®*.

Linking Mission to Money® Grid

High Mission	
A: High Mission, Unprofitable	B: High Mission, Profitable
Unprofitable	**Profitable**
C: Low Mission, Unprofitable	D: Low Mission, Profitable
Low Mission	

In the chart the vertical axis measures how relatively important each activity is to the nonprofit's mission. The horizontal axis measures the profitability or unprofitability of that activity. Each activity will be represented by a dot on the chart. For-profit businesses will have activities only in Quadrant B, which are profitable and closely tied to their brand. They may also have activities in Quadrant D, which are profitable but may not be closely tied to their main business.

Nonprofits exist because no one else will perform activities in Quadrant A, which serve significant community needs but cannot be performed profitably. Every nonprofit will have at least one activity in Quadrant A. But nonprofits cannot operate at losses, so the number of activities on the left side of the chart must be limited. This permission to lose money on an activity must not be seen as a license to operate the program inefficiently or to tolerate bad business practices. Nonprofits must ensure all transactions are competitively bid and that any related party transactions demonstrate arm's length or more favorable pricing. Excessive salaries for staff or board members, overly costly office facilities, or travel or entertainment that cannot be clearly connected with and justified with respect to service delivery are not reasons to be in Quadrants A or C and therefore are considered inappropriate for nonprofits (so-called private benefit issues are now a major focus of IRS Form 990 reports).

One way to limit the number of unprofitable activities is for nonprofits to consider the reduction, elimination, or major restructuring of any activity in Quadrant C because it loses money but does not have a strong link to mission.

The other way to remain viable is to be sure to have sufficient activities in Quadrants B and D. Ideally, the plot of activities of an effective nonprofit will fall in quadrants A, B, and D and will have a pattern that moves up (higher mission) as it moves to the left (lower profit or higher loss).

A nonprofit providing profitable services is not bad or greedy or dishonest; it is doing what is necessary. For example, nonprofit hospitals usually lose money in their emergency rooms and obstetric wards, as well as on charity care for uninsured patients (Quadrant A). They usually remain financially viable by making money in their cardiac and orthopedic wards and on their privately insured patients (Quadrant B). Museums often lose money on their permanent exhibits (Quadrant A), but make money on gift shops and private events (Quadrant D).

The choice and mix of profitable and unprofitable activities is a critical policy decision of the board so it is essential to know which of the organization's activities run profits, which are self-supporting, and which lose money. Looking at the organization in this way dramatically alters how one thinks about each activity's goals and prospects. It may even alter how one views the mission, priorities, and long-term financial plan of the organization.

The most practical way to stay on top of the mix of profitable and unprofitable activities is right at the budget building stage: organize the budget so that the revenues for a specific activity are juxtaposed to the expenses for that same activity in a manner that lets the organization budget for an organization-wide profit as shown in the following table. In this example, Activity One runs significant profits to offset losses in Activities Two and Three.

Example of a Budget Organized by Activity

	Total Organization	Activity 1	Activity 2	Activity 3
Revenue	42	25	13	4
Expense	(39)	(10)	(15)	(14)
Profit/(Loss)	3	15	(2)	(10)

Nonprofit leaders should carefully review the relative importance to mission of the three activities so that they can locate each activity in one of the quadrants of the Linking Mission to Money® Grid. The board should explicitly approve running large losses in Activity Three only if the activity is high mission, falling in Quadrant A. Similarly it should confirm that Activity One is the lowest mission of the three and that Activity Two falls in between. If this is not the case, review the purpose and financial structure of the activities.

If calculating profit and loss by activity is new to the organization, start doing so in a simple manner by using the accounting detail already available (by department for example) and don't try to assign personnel or purchases to more than one activity. Once comfortable with think-ing, setting policy, and monitoring in this simple profit/loss manner, consider getting more sophisticated. The first step in that direction is to start to assign each staff member to an activity, and to multiple activities where appropriate by estimating percentages (possibly by polling staff) to attri-bute to each activity. Allocating a percentage of the execu-tive director's salary across multiple activities is an example of this cost-allocation method. The next step in sophisti-cation is to start allocating all facility and administrative overhead costs across all activities (accounting, utilities, ex-ecutive staff, board expenses, etc.). Calculating building operating cost per square foot and allocating square feet of space to each activity is one way to assign facility costs. When this is done in fairly complete detail, it is called *cost accounting*. One may want to do this at some point, but there is little value to the added expense of cost accounting until the leadership of the nonprofit are ready to set policy and make budget decisions based on whether they want a particular activity to be run at a profit or at a loss.

If a nonprofit organization does not provide some ser-vices that earn profits, then very closely and skeptically re-view its financial structure. Become convinced that it is not implicitly staking its future on the luck of having reliable large donors or grantors year after year. If it is not allowing profit-making, the nonprofit is taking risks with its ability to sustain services.

9. AN EXAMPLE OF A BUDGET APPROACH FOR A STRATEGICALLY FOCUSED BOARD

There are many approaches to and theories about budgeting. Choose one that fits with the time and expertise the board and staff have available, which may vary over time. The technique and complexity of the approach to a budget is less important than the objective of a budget: to identify priorities and have a plan of action that can be followed over a twelve-month period that will achieve the nonprofit's priorities by the end of the budget year.

The ideal budget process from a board perspective is one that keeps the board's focus on strategic decisions. At the staff level, there are myriad details that must be examined, but such details can be distracting to the board. The board is critical for two basic decisions:

1. What are we going to do next year that is different from what we are doing this year and why are we making this change?

2. Is budget surplus, deficit, or balance appropriate for next year, and how should we achieve that?

Most budget detail is not germane to these two decisions. An effective budget process emphasizes for the board that portion of detail that is relevant to these two decisions. For example, the majority of the lines in the budget are not relevant to what the nonprofit proposes to change because most activities will continue from year to year with little change, and there are virtually no policy or strategic issues to confront in budgeting for unchanging activities.

Rather, it is a smaller number of budget lines, reflecting changing activities that link to the strategic plan, that are relevant to board decision-making. Similarly, the budget-balance decision requires one to know only the bottom line and the special events that need to occur for the staff estimates of major revenues and expenses to be realized, as discussed in Chapter 7 on conservative budgeting.

In working with my clients I have found that these two decisions are best informed by an approach that I call *continuation and initiative budgeting*. This approach separates information on continuing, unchanging activities from information on the special efforts that are being proposed to advance or modify delivery of the mission. This approach can allow the board to focus on whether it wishes to advance or modify the mission and whether the special efforts are financially or programmatically desirable. The following table is an example of the summary page of a proposed budget that would be presented to a board that used continuation and initiative budgeting.

	Proposed Budget	Ref
ONGOING ANNUAL ACTIVITIES		
Revenues	$80	a
Fees	$20	b
Grants	$30	c
Gifts	$30	d
Expenses	($63)	e
Personnel	($40)	f
Non-personnel	($23)	g
Ongoing Net Revenues	$17	h
INITIATIVES AND SPECIAL PROJECTS		
Restricted Fund Project (net revenue)	$3	j
New Training Program	($15)	k
Additional Center	($30)	l
Outreach to Teenagers	($5)	m
Total Initiatives and Special Projects	($47)	n
Surplus/(Deficit)	**($30)**	p
(Add)/Withdraw Reserves, Cash Balances	**$30**	q

This budget proposal distinguishes between the revenues and expenses related to ongoing, unchanging activities (items a through h) and the special efforts being proposed to meet the goals and priorities the board chose at the beginning of the budget cycle (items j through m). Items p and q reveal the staff's proposal to balance this budget through use of existing reserves. If the program can be broken down into major profitable and unprofitable activities, there should be a similar table presented for each major activity.

Board deliberation on this budget would focus almost entirely on the initiatives (j through m), on the proposed deficit (item p and its component surpluses and deficits for each major activity), and on the method to fund the deficit (item q). These board deliberations may conclude that the use of reserves needs to be modified (item q), the number or size of the initiatives needs to be reduced (item n), some ongoing activities need to be scaled back (items f and g), ongoing revenues need to be expanded (items b, c, and d), or some combination of all the above. Every proposal to modify any ongoing revenue or expense would be reported back to the board as a new initiative because it would represent changes that merit closer scrutiny by the board than a continuation activity requires.

The difference between a continuing item and an initiative is subjective. Here are some examples: The personnel in the **continuation** budget should be the personnel the nonprofit has today, including vacant positions. If the budget proposes a staff member to do largely what he or she did last year (and that task is not part of a multi-year initiative from the year before), then the position is in the continuation budget. On the other hand, if the budget proposes that the person do something very different than what he or she is doing now, then there should be two entries in the budget:

the continuation budget will include the current activities and the initiative form will describe the new activity she will do and any current activities that will be dropped. The initiative form will report a net zero cost if there are no spending or revenue implications of the initiative.

Another example can be found in the case of advertising. The distinction between ongoing advertising expenses and advertising initiatives rests on the answers to these questions: What advertising is routine? What advertising is a new approach? What advertising specifically advances a goal and priority?

The distinction one should be seeing is that an **initiative** is something entirely different from what is being done today and it is targeted to specific institutional goals and priorities set by the board earlier in the budget cycle. An initiative starts at a specific time, calls for specific people and things, and produces a specific result. It may be finite or it may continue into future years, thus playing a key role in harnessing the budget process to carry out change over several years. When the change is finally complete, it will become part of future continuation budgets.

Some initiatives will redirect existing resources to achieve a new end so that the initiative can be carried out at zero net cost. Or there may be an initiative that actually makes money, as found in item j on the chart. It is likely that most initiatives will have a net cost because they may require additional people and purchases of goods or services, while bringing in no net revenues (items k, l, m). What is key is that each initiative is clearly tied to a specific goal <u>and</u> priority identified in the planning process.

An initiative is put together like a multi-year mini-budget for a project: it has a proposal, timeline, deliverables, estimated expenses and ways to pay for them, and a clear statement of which board goals are addressed and which constituencies will benefit. In managing institutional change over several budget years, the initiative approach provides a tool to follow an activity easily from year to year and to evaluate its progress and achievements in isolation from the rest of the budget At the end of this chapter is an example of a form the executive director could distribute to staff to use to provide all this information for their initiative proposals. Staff members would fill out the form and prepare a spreadsheet detailing the revenues and expenses for each initiative.

Remember, the purpose of a budget is to help leaders make informed decisions. The budget proposal needs to make clear what is routine or unchanging, and at the same time highlight where there are choices to make.

Criteria for Budget Decisions

Most of the time spent in reviewing the budget should be spent in reviewing the initiatives. There are three criteria that make for an ideal initiative to approve:

- The initiative clearly links multiple goals and/or priorities.

- The initiative has a "big bang for the buck"; that is, a large impact on priorities and goals with a modest cost.

- The initiative has a high probability of being successful and showing concrete results before the end of the fiscal year.

The entire organization benefits if it can show that its strategic planning is making a difference. Toward that end, the board should favor initiatives that make a significant difference in several high priority areas sooner rather than later.

Once the board has determined which initiatives have merit, it begins the back and forth between how it wishes to balance the budget and how many initiatives it wishes to undertake for the coming year. Remember, this is not just a financial decision. It is also a decision concerning how staff should spend their time, how well the organization can absorb change, and how successfully the organization can phase out some ongoing activities in order to accommodate new initiatives.

The appeal of this continuation and initiative approach to budgeting is that it makes it much easier for the board to know where to spend its time in reviewing the proposed budget. If a nonprofit has a good sense of its mission, goals, and priorities, this approach is worth testing for the next budget round.

INITIATIVE PROPOSAL FORM

Don't forget to submit your initiative spreadsheet with this form.

Name of Initiative:

Staff Implementing (underline staff member whose spreadsheet contains this proposal):

Institutional Priority Addressed:

Goal Addressed:

Description of Initiative
- How will this advance institutional priorities?
- What outcome do you expect and how will this be measured?
- How do you plan to get there (when, with what)?
- Who are the stakeholders involved in implementation?
- Which stakeholders will benefit after implementation?

Description of Resources Needed

Personnel:

Other Expenses:

Revenues added or continuation budget expenses shifted or reduced:

Net estimated cost this year:

Net estimated cost the following year:

Milestones
[These milestone entries should match the timing in your spreadsheet and be by month or quarter. Milestones should be provided for hires, major purchases, initial deliverables, final deliverables, etc.]

[To download a copy of this form, go to www.linkingmissiontomoney.com/LMMforms]

Key Questions on Mission-Focused Budgets

1. Can you place each of your activities onto the Linking Mission to Money® grid?

2. Have you established priorities for the year that are clearly reflected in your budget decisions?

3. Does your budget allocate resources in a way that ensures progress consistent with your strategic plan?

4. Are your budget decisions "conserve-ative" so that mission is sustainable and the highest priority activities are preserved or enhanced?

◈ SECTION III ◈
LEADING A MISSION-FOCUSED BOARD

T he board has worked hard over the years to assemble a membership that brings diverse skills and perspectives to the table, but diversity has value only to the extent that it is drawn upon. The structure of meetings and the tone set for board discussions are the key determinants of how that diversity is utilized.

Board meetings can be filled with endless presentations, brief committee reports, and votes that are mere formalities. Board meetings frequently have too little informed discussion. How many questions were board members able to ask in the last meeting before the time keeper signaled for the next item on the agenda? And, unfortunately, some boards may actually frown on members who ask questions and "slow down the meeting."

I urge all nonprofit leaders to consciously examine the culture of the board to see if it is one that encourages questions and values diverse perspectives.

- Are there board members who say nothing during a meeting?

- Are board members' doubts, concerns, or worries about a strategy, policy, or course of action actively sought?

- Do each member's opinions get known and does each member have a sufficient understanding of the issue at hand and its importance to the organization?

I can hear the groan: "Oh, those meetings will be end-less." They don't have to be if the meeting has a predeter-mined purpose and goal and if necessary information and background is distributed to members in advance of the meeting. Before the next board meeting, ask what is the actual purpose of the meeting. It may be surprising to conclude that the pre-determined purpose is just to have the meeting: the board meets quarterly, the executive committee meets monthly, the annual meeting is in September, etc.

Why meet unless there is a purpose? I believe the purpose of a board meeting is to tap the perspective, experience, and relationships of the board members to address key issues and challenges which the staff identify. Working together, the executive director and board chair should fill the meeting schedules in advance with the major strategic and planning issues that are identified. For this to be productive and successful the leadership must also resolve to foster a culture that welcomes questions and values diverse and divergent opinions. If the board always agrees, has little discussion or debate, and follows agendas that are fairly predictable, the meetings aren't providing much value to the organization nor making the best use of the time that board members and staff have made available.

In this section we discuss the core issues to monitor each month and the need for questioning by the board in order to see beyond to what the numbers reveal. Understanding comes from questioning in an attitude of support of and partnership with the executive director and staff.

If the board meets less often than monthly, financial reports should provide background on mission and recent experience. Good reports should start with a reminder of past revenue and expenditure trends relative to the current budget, as well as a brief summary of top priority goals and projects in the budget and how they are meeting progress milestones. If the reports the board receives don't work for any member of the board, insist that they be changed; if one member doesn't understand them, most of the other board members probably don't understand them either.

Board oversight of budget execution should emphasize the fact that the organization's strategy and priorities need to be achieved. The numbers should help and inform that conversation, but they are not sufficient by themselves. To focus oversight on the key priorities, initiatives, and time-tables for the year one needs to be reminded what they are. The best reports from the staff will be the ones that prompt probing questions about priorities, mission, and focus.

Define a successful board meeting as one that puts current or emerging problems on the table for open discussion and resolution. Regularly use meetings to assure that the organization's activities remain consistent with its mission and current priorities. Scan board members' eyes during a meeting to see where confusion or concern may appear and be sure no board member still has that look by the time the meeting ends. If this is done, the board will be more engaged, they will view each meeting as an opportunity to make a positive contribution, and the staff who attend will regard each meeting as a helpful time to overcome problems.

10. ORGANIZING THE BOARD

Often referred to under the umbrella term of *governance*, the question of the division of labor among board, staff, board chair, and executive director has no perfect answer. I have seen board structures that worked for a year or two but then became unworkable when just one board member changed. Rather than get bogged down in a discussion of the myriad possible ways to organize, I focus on the roles that I think are most necessary in order to attract and retain committed and talented staff and board members.

Three Critical Board Duties

The board has three major tasks:

1. to set and sustain the strategic direction and policies of the organization;

2. to support and encourage the executive director in maintaining the financial health and effective management of the organization; and

3. to confirm execution of the policies, strategies, and priorities of the organization.

These three tasks don't overlap very well and sometimes result in contradictory behavior, particularly with respect to oversight. To help focus most easily on these duties, in the following table I have highlighted for each one essential activity and one representative question.

In previous chapters I talked about the board's strategic tasks to fulfill the first duty: have a long-term set of goals and mission, formulate a financial plan to sustain those goals, and assemble an annual budget that allocates resources to specific activities to achieve those goals in a stable and sustainable manner. The board's key activity is monitoring the budget in a way that focuses on timely completion of a set of actions that accomplish the top priority goals. Board members will know they are doing this if in every meeting they get a complete answer to the question: "Are we focusing our efforts on our top priorities?" The completeness of the answer will indicate if this is a problem that requires more board attention.

The board's key task in support of staff is to choose a skilled chief executive. After that, an effective board casts itself in the role of seeking to help the executive director, actively soliciting the executive's suggestions as to where the board can be most useful. The board should define its own success to be its ability to foster the success of its executive director. The best way to help the executive director is to focus board activities on planning for the future and anticipating challenges. Board members will know they are doing this if in every meeting they get a complete answer to this question, "Are we accomplishing what we need to accomplish this year?"

The fly in the ointment can easily be the board's third duty, its oversight function. Board oversight is a role that <u>validates</u> principles, objectives, and execution. In contrast, micromanagement is a role that <u>dictates how to execute</u> – and it must be *avoided* by the board in all but the most extreme circumstances.

Board members who are active managers or top executives can easily forget to leave their executive hats at the door and seek to fulfill their board role by acting, doing, or directing as they would in their day job. Oversight can and should be a hands-off activity. Support is an activity that can be hands-on but it should be hands-on only at the request of the executive director. When unsolicited, help can become usurpation, which soon leads to the board's second-guessing the executive director and, before one realizes it, the supportive role of the board can have transformed into direct management by the board. Ironically, boards that are worried about too little to do or too few opportunities to feel engaged are oftentimes in the position of micromanaging because they are neglecting to put enough time into their strategic duties.

The key word in board oversight is *validate*. To validate execution means to ensure that what was supposed to be done was indeed done and that it remains consistent with the organization's principles, objectives, and mission. The action that best accomplishes this with the least tension is an extensive review of the past year, which is discussed more completely in Chapter 14. If the board is slipping into micromanagement, pause and limit discussion to the question, "Are we able to sustain our current level of services for the foreseeable future?"

Oversight is essential and needs to be persistent, by both executive director and board. The mistake is made when management oversight is confused with board oversight. Management oversight is "on the ground" and involves internal controls such as the staff showing up for work, laws being followed, procedures being documented, etc. Board oversight is "40,000 feet up" and involves validating the continued relevance of and need for the organization's mission and ensuring the consistency of policies and principles and the effectiveness of objectives.

Duties	Activities	Questions
1. To set and sustain the strategic financial direction and policies of the organization.	1. Budget oversight: monitoring the completion of your priorities on schedule, on budget, and on objective.	1. Are we focusing our efforts on our top priorities?
2. To support and encourage the executive director in maintaining the financial health and effective financial management of the organization.	2. Planning for the future, both programmatic and financial.	2. Are we accomplishing what we need to accomplish this year?
3. To oversee execution of the financial policies, strategies, and priorities of the organization.	3. Looking back to assess the accuracy and adequacy of staff communication to the board and to assess the effectiveness of your organization's activities in addressing your mission.	3. Are we able to sustain our current level of services for the foreseeable future?

Board Officers and Their Roles

The types and titles of board positions are very flexible and there is little standardization. Set up a structure that fits the personalities and skills of board members in a way that facilitates good decision-making. Most important is making the duties, responsibilities, and authorities clear to everyone, including staff.

Titles of positions should serve the board's needs. Titles can be confusing and get in the way of accomplishing the purposes of a position, even the title of "president." For example, in some organizations the president is the chair of the board and in other organizations the president is the senior staff position, which also can be labeled executive director, chief executive officer, secretary, or managing director, among other titles. Similarly, the titles treasurer and secretary can be used for board or for staff positions. Other common board titles are chair, vice-chair, and director. Many of these titles exist solely because state law requires that signatories on corporate documents have specific titles. Some organizations also use titles as an indirect way of determining membership on an executive committee.

Regardless of the titles selected, there are two roles that should be covered whether or not they are required by state law. First, designate a board member to be responsible for setting agendas, running the meetings, and coordinating with the senior manager (typically this is the chair coordinating with the executive director). Second, designate a board member to be responsible for reporting on the organization's financial condition, coordinating the outside financial audit, and coordinating with the senior financial manager. In larger organizations this is often the treasurer coordinating with the chief financial officer or business manager. These two positions primarily exist to create a clear line of communication between two key staff and the board. If the organization has other key staff positions, consider appointing a board member to act as a single point of contact for that staff member. There needn't be a title for that board duty.

Since I have chosen to highlight the board chair and board treasurer, let me add a few cautions about their responsibilities with respect to the rest of the board. The board chair is responsible for ensuring that clear agendas are set for each board meeting. In addition, it is the board chair's duty to ensure that the board performs its financial oversight and decision-making duties.

Note that I have carefully used the word "ensure" for the chair, not the word "perform": it is not appropriate for the chair to replace or pre-empt the oversight and decision-making duties of other board members. The chair is an organizer and facilitator; the board must not delegate its duties to this one person. In particular the chair should take the lead in encouraging a culture of asking questions, facilitating good decision-making by the board, and keeping abreast with the executive director on execution of board decisions. It is the chair's duty to see that meetings have a purpose, accomplish that purpose, and address each major board duty over the course of the year.

This same caution applies to the role of treasurer. The board treasurer should be a person who is very interested in the finances of the organization. This person does not need to be an accountant or a finance professional, although every nonprofit should try to have someone with those skills on the board. In fact, sometimes it is best to have a non-accountant as the treasurer because a generalist in this position may be better able to facilitate participation by the entire board in the financial oversight and decision-making duties of the board. I have seen too many situations in which the appointment of an accountant or finance professional to the treasurer's post in effect lets the rest of the board "off the hook" for paying attention to the finances and understanding the significant financial issues facing the organization.

Seeing emerging problems is most successfully done with as many eyes watching as possible; beware letting an expert take this responsibility away from the rest of the board. One of the biggest challenges for the regular, "non-financial expert" board member is to persist in asking questions about the finances when the chair and/or treasurer want to move on to other agenda items. Having a non-expert in those positions can often contribute positively to an environment that encourages discussion and questioning by the entire board. The board cannot expect a non-expert by himself to see behind a vague presentation or a confusing table of figures, whereas they may be inclined to leave to an expert the identification and resolution of problems.

Board Committees and Their Roles

There are four activities that should be assigned to committees or a board committee of the whole:

1. Budget oversight: monitoring the completion of priorities on schedule, on budget, and on objective;

2. Planning for the future: both programmatic and financial;

3. Internal communication: assess the accuracy and adequacy of staff communication to the board.

4. Mission impact: assess the effectiveness of the organization's activities in addressing its mission.

Some boards assign several committees to these activities but the chair can easily accomplish them at meetings of the full board through careful agenda planning over the course of the year.

The names and numbers of committees should serve the organization's needs. There are usually no requirements to have any committees, in which case the board will be working as what is called a *committee of the whole*. The only useful purpose for having committees is to divide up the work so that not every board member must devote time to every board task. This can be varied as often as necessary. Some organizations leave the committee structure up to the chair of the board and in fact change numbers, titles, and duties of committees with each new board chair. Other organizations may choose to use only *ad hoc* committees, which by definition are created for a specific purpose and expire when that purpose is achieved. Some common committee titles are executive, audit, budget, finance, program, strategy, personnel, travel, benefits, building, development, acquisitions, and capital.

This list is far from exhaustive but it should provide assurance that a board can do whatever best meets its needs and give a committee whatever name best suits its purposes. I will describe the most essential committee roles and name them finance, executive, and audit, but choose different names if appropriate.

In large or complex organizations the first of the four financial activities – budget oversight – is often assigned to a <u>finance committee</u>. This committee will be expected to provide more timely oversight and decision-making by meeting more frequently than the full board can meet.

The second activity of programmatic and financial planning can be assigned to a planning committee or to the <u>executive committee</u> in order to keep things moving along. If this duty is delegated to a committee I encourage keeping the full board firmly engaged in planning with at least one stand-alone board meeting per year devoted exclusively to reviewing programmatic and financial plans.

The last two activities are often assigned to the executive committee or the <u>audit committee</u>. Audit committees are commonly created to ensure that the organization systematically evaluates the quality and integrity of its accounting and financial statements and internal controls. The audit committee can also be used to provide a confidential forum for evaluation of concerns regarding staff or board misconduct. *This function is the sole exception to the rule that the board should stay out of detailed operational issues.*

Unfortunately, too often the audit committee is limited solely to approving the annual financial audit. (The specifics of the annual financial audit will be discussed in Chapter 14.) This duty of assessment and review can be more effective with an expanded role. Ask this committee, or another the board selects, to extend its review to include the organization's financial health, internal communication, and fulfillment of goals and mission.

Internal communication to the board by staff should regularly be reviewed for its effectiveness. It is in this area that persistent questioning can be most helpful. If board meetings become too routine and largely formulaic, it is worthwhile every so often to take a skeptical look at the reports staff prepare to discern if the board is getting substance. A board culture that "punishes the messenger" or in any way sends an implicit or explicit message that bad news is not welcome is particularly vulnerable to staff reporting that skirts substance in order to avoid tension. This review of internal communication is not commonly done because it offers the possibility of creating tension and stress. Better to have some occasional tension and stress than a board that is out of touch.

In a small organization, the fourth activity – objective assessment by the board – may be more difficult because of multiple overlapping oversight and managerial roles that board members may play. In these cases, the board may need to have an outside auditor play an expanded evaluation role. If the services of an outside auditor are prohibitively expensive for the organization, consider asking an audit firm to help *pro bono*, or seek a donor to support the cost. If either option is not feasible, ask another, trusted local organization to evaluate the organization's financial health and its focus on mission. While this last option may seem awkward or embarrassing at first, the insight and objective information provided by outside, confidential review is worth its weight in gold.

However the organization chooses to organize its board and assign roles and responsibilities, it is essential that it remain keenly aware of how and why it is doing things the way it does. In Chapter 14, "Conducting a Meaningful Annual Check-up" I will talk more about how the board should regularly ask itself if responsibility and accountability are clearly assigned. In addition, perhaps an orientation of new members can provide a useful vehicle both to compel review of the organization's ways of doing business and to foster probing questions of those ways by the new board members.

11. BOARD MEETINGS: FOCUSING ON MISSION ACHIEVEMENT

I t is important to keep board members engaged and focused on how they can support the nonprofit. The board meeting is the primary opportunity to maintain that engagement. If a board meets monthly for three hours, meetings provide only 36 hours per year to achieve that engagement. Many boards meet less often. That is a very limited amount to time, so how it is used is critical. The combination of effective reporting by the staff and probing questioning by the board is the best method to keep on top of the budget during the year and to make sure that emerging problems are flagged without having to get involved in operational micromanagement.

Unfortunately, too many board meetings are passive listening exercises for board members: they hear presentations, make brief committee reports, and hold votes that are often formalities. For those boards, it is not surprising that attendance flags and quorums become a challenge.

A nonprofit that has recruited talented members to the board knows that they are busy and want their time to be productive and useful. All board members have many demands on their time and many alternative uses for the time a board meeting demands. Questions they ask themselves to determine if they will clear their schedules for the next board meeting are:

1. What is the purpose of the meeting?

2. What will be the main accomplishment of the meeting?

3. What can a board member do to prepare for the meeting?

A good agenda is a powerful tool to make it clear that the next meeting will address all three board duties discussed in the previous chapter. It also signals that decisions will be made that will benefit from attendance by every board member. Consider using the agenda structure in the following illustration. Distribute the agenda far enough in advance so that it can influence board members' scheduling decisions.

An Agenda to Address Three Critical Board Duties at Each Meeting

A. Financial status (dashboard of critical risks)

    1. Cash available; projected cash flow for next few months

    2. Status of unpaid bills

    3. Status of collection of outstanding pledges

    4. Projected year-end results

B. Follow up on board assignments from last meeting (to support and encourage staff in maintenance of financial health)

C. Progress on fiscal year priorities/initiatives/action assignments (to oversee progress)

D. Review of one key strategic issue or policy (part of an annual cycle to set and sustain strategy)

Adjourn

My recommended agenda has four parts. The first is an initial quick scan of key risks so the board can know if special intervention is necessary. I will elaborate on this more in the next section.

The second part focuses on the second key duty of a board: to support the executive director and staff in maintaining the financial health of the organization. Nonprofits need help in making contacts, finding vendors, getting second opinions, and raising money. At every board meeting, one or more board members should be given an assignment that helps the nonprofit, and each meeting should follow up on those assignments. A board member's knowing he has to do something after this meeting and that he will be asked to report on his progress at the next meeting provides a strong signal to that board member that he is useful and that he had better attend the next meeting.

The third part is a structured way to oversee the execution of the year's major projects and initiatives and their continued relevance to the sustainability of the organization. If the nonprofit has used the initiative budget format presented in Chapter 9, this part of the agenda will be easy to assemble. It sends a strong signal to the staff that the priorities of the year will get close board attention. It provides an incentive for staff to ensure progress is made in each priority area by the next board meeting. It also provides a routine opportunity to ask for board advice and assistance in order to keep those priorities moving ahead. Board assignments may arise from this part of the agenda.

Throughout this book I emphasize the ongoing strategic duties of the board because strategic discussion, debate, and review must not be limited to a special meeting that happens once a year. The last part of the agenda addresses the board's duty to set and sustain the strategy of the organization. I encourage boards to devote at least one agenda item in each board meeting to a discussion of some aspect of mission or strategy.

Mission and strategic direction don't exist in a vacuum. The environment in which an organization operates is constantly changing: the community's needs continually change,

the profile and needs of clients or patrons change, the economic climate changes. Considering all that change, why
would one allow the organization's strategy and mission to
become carved in stone? A board member's most valuable
contribution is his vision of what the community currently
needs and how the organization's mission can be adapted to
best address those needs.

With this type of agenda, each meeting will be meaningful, decisions will be made in a timely manner, and board
members will see that their time and skills are useful and
utilized.

Notice that finances have not been a large part of this discussion. The progress of programs, the solution to problems,
and the refinement of strategy have been the focus. Finance
is important but its importance lies in its ability to reveal
problems effectively. I suggest making it a quick review using a very short report, often called a dashboard. Any board
discussion of finances would be contingent on whether the
dashboard suggests problems are emerging.

Key Components of a Financial Health Dashboard

The concept of a dashboard is that a small set of key in-
dicators of financial health are often reported with a special
symbol or color code associated with the staff's interpretation of that indicator. Often the color code is red for items
that suggest immediate difficulties, yellow for emerging
difficulties, and green for areas of no current concern. In
general, if the colors are red or yellow, the board should immediately begin discussion of that indicator, its implications,
and the steps the staff suggest be taken. Most often the colors will be green and the board should quickly move on to
the next item on the agenda.

In the financial review at the start of each meeting, there
are four items to be sure to focus on:

1. The top priority for the year is on schedule.

2. The key activities and initiatives in the budget are occurring in the way and on the schedule that the budget anticipated.

3. The categories of bills that have been received but not paid by the end of the month (payables), such as payroll taxes, unemployment insurance, workers compensation, and retirement contributions that are owed.

4. The amount of cash the organization has available now and for the next few months, and the major events that could possibly occur in the coming months to make it unable to pay future bills on time (such as cancellations of or delays in cash receipts for major pledges, grants, and other "receivables").

These four points represent the source of most organizational failures, yet they are relatively easy to track. It may be hard to believe that a board's oversight job can boil down to so few things, or that it needs to pay less attention to all the other things, so let's delve a bit deeper.

At the beginning of budget preparation (Chapter 5) the board identified what its primary goal for the coming year would be. The first item a board should always review is whether the organization is on schedule for meeting that goal or if any unforeseen issues with implementation have arisen. Making this item the first on the agenda also keeps it foremost in the mind of the executive director. This emphasis is very helpful for him or her because the disruptions of everyday management can easily distract even the best executive from the priorities set by the board to achieve that mission. But the board—by its more periodic and strategic attention to the organization—can in many circumstances be better equipped to maintain focus on priorities than the operationally focused staff.

The second item in the dashboard identifies slippage of key programs or initiatives, which can harm constituents, mislead donors, violate grant requirements, or erode good-will. There is always a reason for something to slip. The board needs to be on top of this so that remediation can occur and course corrections can be made. If the staff is overcommitted, the board needs to recognize this and rear-range priorities and commitments in a way that is positive and helps the staff to keep the highest priorities on track.

The third item in the dashboard recognizes that juggling is the name of the game in daily management, but, however well intentioned, juggling can go too far. A well-intentioned but disastrous example of juggling is the gradual putting off of paying some bills in order to pay more pressing bills: the payroll is paid but the withholding taxes don't get sent to the IRS; the screaming vendor gets paid but the insurance premium doesn't, and so on. And while the board shouldn't micromanage, the financial report should routinely include how many and which bills weren't paid at the end of each month (payables) and how long those bills have remained unpaid ("aged payables").

It is critical for the board to be sure that the list isn't growing from month to month and that the organization isn't being put at risk by any of the delayed payments. If ei-ther situation is occurring, have a calm, reasoned discussion of how and when these payments are going to get back on track. The board may have to conclude that some activities—maybe even some of its top priorities—need to be canceled or scaled back in order to allow the organization to catch up or stay current with its mission-critical bills.

Lastly, the fourth item in the dashboard points to the tripwire of crisis: running out of cash. Every month the financial report should include key numbers that let the board know the amount of cash that is readily available and other items that will alert it to the need to identify possible future events that could potentially jeopardize operations. Suggested areas in which the organization should develop measures include:

- Are there major pledges that are expected to be paid? What could affect their timely payment?

- Are there major grants that are expected? What could affect their timely payment?

The Board should make sure steps are taken before the next meeting to give better assurance that the cash for these items will be received when expected.

- Is there a major payment due in the coming months?

Again, make sure steps are taken before the next meeting to accumulate enough cash in advance so that payment can be made on time without pushing back payment of other, less critical bills.

12. FINANCIAL REPORTS: LINKING MISSION TO MONEY®

The thorniest dilemma in a board member's life is knowing which practices in the member's day job apply to nonprofits and how much detail is appropriate for board members to get into. On the one hand, board members want to let staff run the organization without micromanagement from the board. On the other hand, responsible board members aren't satisfied with brief and rote recitation of financial numbers at each board meeting. Effective board members want to press the staff without seeming distrustful. They want to feel they have a command of what is going on without making this board seat their second job. They want to find a middle ground, yet sometimes the staff makes that middle ground difficult to find. Some staffs, in order to demonstrate their mastery, want to talk boards through excruciating detail that drags the discussion from the forest down to the twigs. Other staffs, in order to assert independence, give boards minimum information and assert that everything is "on target."

The ideal approach is to do what is necessary to fulfill three duties: to set strategy, support staff, and oversee that the strategy is executed. A board can fulfill its duties by identifying a plan that matches the use of resources to the ability to address and sustain mission, by reviewing operating results that demonstrate that mission priorities are being accomplished, and by supporting staff in keeping the focus at 40,000 feet.

In this chapter we will discuss how to use board members' for-profit skills and experience from their day jobs to set nonprofit strategy and oversee its execution at the level of detail appropriate for a board member.

Setting Strategy

As discussed in Chapter 8, the skills in assessing the profitability of the various activities of a business translate directly into the nonprofit world. It is appropriate to ask staff to isolate the revenues and expenses attributable to the major activities of the nonprofit, including allocating overhead expenses to each activity.

In the for-profit world, the success of an activity is measured primarily by its profitability. Recall in Chapter 8 we had three activities:

- Activity One with a profit of 15

- Activity Two with a loss of 2

- Activity Three with a loss of 10

While a for-profit would restructure or cancel Activities Two and Three because of their continued losses, nonprofits must expand this profit-loss evaluation of value onto the two-dimensional Linking Mission to Money® Grid below. I call this exercise "Locating your dots" and I define strategy as "Moving the dots." In this grid, each activity has a horizontal dimension for profitability, so the three activities range from far left for the large losses of Activity Three to the far right for the large profits of Activity One. For nonprofits, the three activities must also be assigned a vertical dimension that describes how vital and effective they are in fulfilling the nonprofit's mission.

Linking Mission to Money® Grid

	High Mission	
A: High Mission, Unprofitable		B: High Mission, Profitable
Unprofitable		**Profitable**
C: Low Mission, Unprofitable		D: Low Mission, Profitable
	Low Mission	

As discussed in Chapter 8, for-profits have activities only in quadrants B and D, while nonprofits must have at least one activity in Quadrant A. Both for-profits and nonprofits avoid any activities in Quadrant C, which lose money but contribute little to the mission of the organization.

Whether this nonprofit's strategy is sound and is properly linking mission to money depends on the mission relevance of Activities One and Three. In the grid below, the strategy is sound and sustainable.

- The high mission activity is the one losing money

- Lower mission activities lose less money

- Lowest mission activities make money

- The profitable activities earn sufficient profits to completely offset the losses of the high mission activities

Okay: Money and Mission are Linked

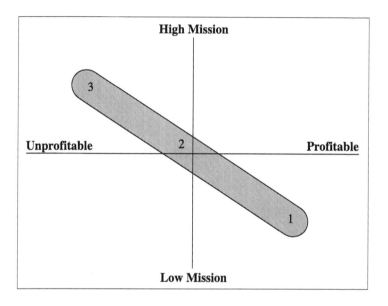

Activity Three is okay even though it loses a good deal of money because it is high mission. In a for-profit, Activity Three would be dropped. In general, when plotting the activities of a nonprofit, there should be a pattern in which the dots move from the upper left to the lower right.

In contrast, the next grid does not show this upper left to lower right pattern. Here, the conflict between for-profit and nonprofit strategy is represented by Activity One. While a for-profit would encourage continuation of Activity One as it is designed, a non-profit is grossly mis-serving its mission by operating its highest mission activity to make substantial profits. It is also mis-serving mission by allowing low-mission Activity Three to absorb its profits.

Not Okay: Money Disconnected from Mission

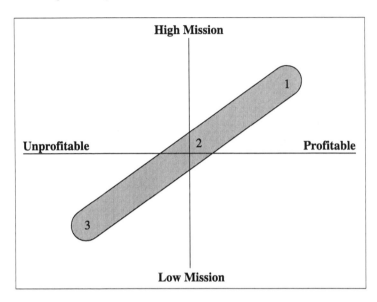

A nonprofit with this grid pattern needs to completely restructure its operations. It is underserving its community's need for Activity One. It could expand offerings beyond what users can pay or donors can support and it should ensure access for those who cannot pay. These types of changes would move the "dot" for Activity One sharply to the left.

In contrast, for Activity Three the nonprofit should totally redesign it to make it more relevant to its community, reprice it to generate sufficient revenues to make a profit, or drop the activity entirely. These three restructuring options would move its "dot" sharply up, move it sharply to the right, or delete the dot entirely, respectively.

Overseeing Adherence to Strategy

In nonprofit finance, the translation of for-profit skills is challenging. Financial statements are the raw materials that financial experts examine to identify clues to what is going on financially in an organization. Unfortunately, financial statements rarely provide an unambiguous view because they are prone to diverse interpretations. For that reason, I don't think they are the appropriate financial reports for a nonprofit board to review.

Financial statements follow rules and formats that are dictated by the Financial Accounting Standards Board (FASB). These rules change regularly and they are complex. They are designed to be rigorous applications of detailed rules so that people trained in financial analysis can more reliably study and compare financial statements across many organizations. Importantly, the rules for nonprofit organizations are different from the rules for for-profit organizations and, while the vocabulary may sound at times like everyday words, they usually have a very precise and sometimes special definition.

The table below is a rough summary of financial terms. Those in the left column are useful in evaluating nonprofit finance while the terms in the right column have no clear meaning in nonprofit finance. Most of the differences are reflected in balance sheet measures, while income statement (P&L, Net change in assets) measures are largely similar. The Glossary at the end of this book provides useful context for a number of these terms.

The first characteristic that distinguishes nonprofit finance from for-profit finance is the limitation on access and usability of some assets. This is represented by the terms board-designated reserves, unrestricted net assets, temporarily restricted net assets, and permanently restricted net assets. Because of this, most financial analysis based on asset ratios does not translate well from for-profit to nonprofit finance.

The second characteristic is that a nonprofit is a trust whose assets must forever remain with a nonprofit. Thus the concept of equity, or an ownership stake in the organization, has no meaning nor do any ratios based on equity have a meaningful interpretation.

Key Terms in Nonprofit Finance	Terms that are not meaningful in Nonprofit Finance
• Working capital reserves	
• Board designated reserves	• Return on equity or on assets
• Unrestricted net assets	• Asset turnover
• Restricted assets	• Financial leverage
• Restricted and unrestricted endowment	• Net equity
• Temporarily restricted assets	• Debt to equity ratio
• Accrual basis	• Debt to assets ratio
• Cash basis	• Market value
• Cash flow	• Earnings yield or ratio
• Budget variance	
• Projected revenues, expenses	
• Earned revenue	
• Contributed revenue	

In Chapter 15 I walk through a set of financial statements to show how to use them to generate good questions. I don't want readers to try to master the statements but rather to confirm what they may already feel: the statements are complex, prone to misinterpretation, and in many ways divergent from the information a board member needs to know to fulfill his responsibilities as a board member.

Going through financial statements is not easy, and the primary outcome is often just to wonder what was going on and what bearing that might have on mission and the sustainability of services. These difficulties can exclude many board members from participating in this review. Some may feel excluded because they dislike financial discussions or because they find them too difficult to understand or to follow. Others may be excluded because extensive questioning makes them feel like they are cast in the role of being suspicious or distrustful of the staff. And others may be excluded because they feel marginalized by the more active and enthusiastic discussion by the financial experts on the board.

There are better and more effective ways for a board member to routinely review and understand nonprofit finances than to examine the standard financial statements. One way is by establishing a set of reports that are routine but focused on helping board members to fulfill their primary duties as a board: to make sure that the organization's priorities, as reflected in the initiatives budget, are being carried out <u>correctly and on schedule</u>. To move in that direction requires redefining the form and purpose for the reports the board receives.

Reports that focus on assessment and corrective action should form the backbone of the board's oversight and decision-making process. For the report on the overall budget, the following simple table should be sufficient. I talked earlier about using the initiatives approach to assembling a budget. This approach assembled two budgets: a continuation budget that updated costs and revenues for ongoing activities and an initiatives budget that incorporated projects and specific actions for the year to achieve the nonprofit's top priorities. This budget approach also makes oversight easier by making oversight of the ongoing operations routine and allowing most of a board's time to be devoted to reporting on achievement of the initiatives the board has approved. The combination of a narrative on initiatives progress with this highly summarized financial table provides a good balance for board oversight.

A Sample Format for a Summary Financial Table

	Fiscal Year 2010-2011 Board Approved Budget	Nov-10 Projected Budget	Net Effective Change from Budget
OPERATIONAL REVENUE			
Earned Revenue	$496,900	$416,932	($79,968)
Grants	$547,300	$463,000	($84,300)
Contributions	$115,800	$2,100	($113,700)
TOTAL OPERATIONAL REVENUE	**$1,160,000**	**$882,032**	**($277,968)**
OPERATIONAL EXPENSES			
Total Salaries and Benefits	$650,800	$6630,800	($20,000)
Total Non-Salaried Operations	$588,291	$546,303	($41,988)
Other Expenses	$4,700	$4,100	($600)
TOTAL EXPENSES	**$1,243,791**	**$1,181,203**	**($62,588)**
NET OPERATING INCOME	**($83,791)**	**($299,171)**	**($340,556)**

Note, I am not limiting my use of the reports to see whether the priorities are being carried out on budget because budget numbers are just one component of a plan. The budget ideally was based on providing a specific level of service delivery that was in turn converted into estimates of monthly service delivery, whether in terms of attendance, clients served, centers opened, training programs delivered, or whatever is the appropriate measure of what the nonprofit intended to accomplish this year. Therefore, the reports should always, as the most important component, have an assessment of how the organization is doing against each of these estimates. For any area that is diverging from the estimates, there should be a recommendation for remediation from the staff that prompts a decision from the board. That decision can be to take an action, to seek further information, or to do nothing. If staff can't provide a good assessment, the board should be concerned and should probe further. Just remember, one can look at numbers and still be missing some significant information.

This approach to board financial reports is based on the fundamental principle of comparative advantage; that is, people should focus on tasks that use their strongest skills. The staff is better at delving into detail and daily operational issues; the board is better at maintaining focus on priorities and on mission delivery and sustainability because it has the perspective and judgment of a concerned observer not caught up in the minutiae of daily management. The financial data are just one piece of information the board should use in fulfilling this role.

In Chapter 18 I talk about the extreme circumstances in which the board may have to violate this division of labor and move into operational details. But such circumstances are not common and a board should generally be wary if it finds itself spending time analyzing numbers and trying to understand accounting rules at the expense of sitting back to review and discuss mission and how effectively it is being accomplished.

13. IDENTIFYING PROBLEMS WITHOUT MICROMANAGING

I hope the previous chapter was persuasive that one should be wary of complex financial statements and should insist on financial reports and tables that are understandable. Remember that a budget is a plan of action that happens to be expressed in terms of numbers, outcomes, and time-tables. The board provides oversight that the execution of the budget is following that plan of action. Financial reports in whatever form, however, cannot be a substitute for think-ing and asking probing questions.

Let's look at a couple of examples of typical budget execu-tion problems and how one can spot these problems without going through the excruciating detail that is appropriate for staff to review but not board members. A highly summarized table and a narrative on the progress of a plan of action are valuable substitutes for a conventional, detailed year-to-date financial report.

Consider a grant-funded program that is budgeted at a certain amount but currently behind schedule. The or-ganization received a $6,000 grant to provide training over three months. The grant proposal requested $3,000 to rent facilities for the training sessions, $1,000 for food, $1,000 for materials, and about $1,000 more for overtime for staff (regular salaries were not part of the grant request.) Nothing has happened over those three months and failure to spend the money will result in forfeiture of the grant. The highly summarized table below has sufficient detail to describe this situation.

Budget Table For A Grant Behind Schedule

	Actual	Plan	Variance Fav/(Unfav)	Percent of Year
Operating revenues	532,650	532,650	**$0**	25%
Fees	370,150	370,150	0	25%
Grants	162,500	162,500	0	25%
Operating expenses	(504,125)	(510,125)	**$6,000**	
Rent	(73,519)	(76,519)	3000	24%
Equip	(49,013)	(51,013)	2000	24%
Personnel	(381,594)	(382,594)	1000	25%
Net revenues	28,525	22,525	**$6,000**	

This report uses only two revenue categories, fees and grants, and only three expense categories, rent, payments for office equipment and supplies, and personnel expenses. The columns tell where the organization is relative to the budget plan. For example, $162,500 was expected to be received in grants in the first quarter (the plan column) and indeed that exact amount was received (the actual column) so that the variance is zero (the variance column). Therefore, one would conclude that the $6,000 grant has been received on time. The first quarter grant revenue was 25 percent of the total amount expected for the full year (the % of year column).

Under expenses, the unspent amounts for rent, food, materials, and overtime under the grant show up on the report but they are about one percent of total spending—a fairly small figure relative to the size of the organization. Oftentimes, one looks just at the percentage expended: 25% of the year is over so about 25% of the budget should have been spent. These percentages are pretty close to target.

Ideally the board would know from looking at this table that the grant would be in jeopardy unless spending were increased. But it is also possible that this minor variance will not raise any flags and the board will leave with the following incorrect conclusion based on just the numbers:

> "Net revenues show we had a good first quarter. Gross revenues are on target and gross expenses are not running over budget, showing we have good control over our spending."

Without probing questions and follow-up, even correct financial reports can be misleading or can be misinterpreted. If, on the other hand, the budget was composed of initiatives including this training program, one would have a ready-made board agenda to review the status of all budgeted initiatives (see Chapter 11 for a discussion of board agendas). The narrative that would accompany this type of budget approach would have reported the lack of progress on this training initiative, thereby making the problem readily apparent.

Alternatively, the board could request that it receive a regular report of revenues and expenses categorized by program. This type of highly summarized report, shown below, is even more effective in highlighting the status of the training program.

A Program-Based Financial Report

	Actual	Plan	Variance Fav/(Unfav)	Percent of year
Net Training	6,000	0	**$6,000**	
Grants	6,000	6,000	0	100%
Expenses	0	(6,000)	6,000	0%
Net Ongoing Operations	22,525	22,525	**$ -**	
Revenues	526,650	526,650	0	100%
Expenses	(504,125)	(504,125)	0	100%

Since the way one identifies and reacts to problems is so important, let's examine another example. This same organization is planning to open three new centers in July, September, and November. In the first quarter (July through September), expected costs are $30,000 for space rental ($15,000 for six months due at occupancy), $20,000 for furniture and equipment ($10,000 in the first month of opening a new center), and $32,000 for additional staff (2 people per center at $4,000 per month per person). As of October, no centers have been opened. Here's a highly summarized first quarter financial report:

A Financial Report Showing Delays in Opening New Centers

Once again, the "expense savings" clearly appear on the report. Would the percentages raise any flags? Would the reader of this report be relieved that personnel costs are under budget? Would one connect this underspending with the fact that two centers have not been opened and no new staff put in place? Would this table help a board realize that there is a service crisis in the organization?

	Actual	Plan	Variance Fav/(Unfav)	Percent of year
Operating revenues	532,650	532,650	**$0**	25%
Fees	370,150	370,150	0	25%
Grants	162,500	162,500	0	25%
Operating expenses	(428,125)	(510,125)	**$82,000**	
Rent	(46,519)	(76,519)	30,000	15%
Equip	(31,013)	(51,013)	20,000	15%
Personnel	(350,594)	(382,594)	32,000	23%
Net revenues	104,525	22,525	**$82,000**	

There will be the greatest likelihood of picking up on this problem if the regular board agenda prompts probing questions based on overseeing that the initiatives for the year are proceeding correctly and on schedule. Simply focusing on whether spending or revenues are "on budget" is often not sufficient in helping to spot emerging problems before they become major issues. At the same time, asking the staff to explain every variance in the budget will involve the board in too great a level of detail that may not be germane to strategic as opposed to operating issues. By focusing reporting on progress and performance of initiatives and overall budget balance, the board will maintain its focus on strategic issues and make the best use of its limited time.

I have focused these examples on the expense side. Crises often are driven by revenue shortfalls in ticket sales, fundraising, and other means of acquiring revenue, but that worry too often can lead boards to develop a counterproductive mandate that spending needs to be kept below budget. Hopefully, these examples have shown that spending below budget can be just as harmful to purpose and mission as having income below budget.

Detailed tables would not have made it easier to spot these problems and more likely they would have made it harder and plunged the board into micromanagement. Even highly summarized tables by themselves should not be relied upon as the sole source of information; only probing questions and narratives can tell the full story.

The best questions a board member can ask will focus on the 40,000 foot, strategic level where a board can be most helpful and effective:

- What are the priorities for the year and have they changed?

- What is the emphasis of actual budget spending?

- Is actual spending still consistent with priorities?

- Are priorities for the year being executed as expected?

- What course corrections are necessary to ensure the organization meets its priorities for the year?

Though a few numbers are critical to getting the story straight, it is important to remember that no one joins a board just to balance the budget but rather to facilitate the achievement of programmatic priorities.

Board oversight of budget execution should emphasize the fact that strategy and priorities need to be achieved. The numbers should help and inform that conversation, but they are not sufficient by themselves. The best reports from the staff will be the ones that prompt probing questions about priorities, mission, and focus.

14. CONDUCTING A MEANINGFUL ANNUAL CHECK-UP

E ven when keeping up with the organization through the budget process and monthly budget reviews, at least once a year it is time to review some basics. Even when an individual feels healthy, if he is wise he still gets a regular physical check-up with his doctor. Similarly, organizations need regular check-ups. Too often, however, this check-up is a discussion limited to the audit committee and a perfunctory presentation by an outside auditor.

This discussion is best done at a special meeting of the full board, ideally around the beginning of each fiscal year. Regard it as the annual validation that the organization understands and is telling its story correctly. This is not an investigation or critical review. It is a supportive inquiry by the board and staff together that is intended to reaffirm on a routine basis that the organization continues to have a sustainable mission with a solid foundation for stable service delivery.

Below are five key areas that should be well understood by everyone on the board. Additional areas can be added. In each area I provide questions to help structure the discussion.

How Much Cash Is Enough?

Adequate cash is essential to the smooth functioning of any organization and cash problems are usually the first sign that some changes may be needed. Cash is the checkbook of the organization; know how the organization will pay its bills on time without bouncing any checks.

- How much cash is it supposed to have on hand?

- What is the action plan if/when cash falls below that level?

- If there are donor requirements that have not yet been met, has the organization set aside the cash needed to fulfill those requirements?

- Last year, did the organization put off paying any bills or paying any taxes because it was short of cash?

- Did it borrow during the year in order to have enough cash?

- How much current cash is from subscriptions, memberships, or tuition, whose parallel expenses are yet to be incurred?

- Are there any lawsuits or grants that are being questioned that might result in forfeiture of some cash?

This list of questions is long in order to provide a flavor of what kind of rocks can lie hidden below quiet waters. Make sure to check below the surface at least once a year, no matter how embarrassing or awkward this process may be. It will be more awkward if the organization founders on rocks that could easily have been avoided.

How Was the Last Budget Balanced?

The best way to know how stable and sustainable finances are is to start peeling the onion to see what's inside. Hopefully, the budget was balanced last year, but there are many ways to balance a budget. The most reliable form of balance is for routine revenues to equal or exceed expenditures. (In Chapter 16 I will end with a discussion of the limitations of using endowment funds as a stable routine income source. The ability to borrow or to obtain extraordinary gifts can also be illusory, especially during hard times.)

- Did revenue equal or exceed expenditures after excluding any use of endowment income or principal, any use of borrowing, and any exceptional (one-time) gifts?

If the answer is no, revisit the financial plan and look for ways to start building the types of reserves discussed in Chapter 16 "Tools for Sustainability." Also examine current revenue sources and the list of expenditures to see if the organization can build up the former and slow down growth of the latter over the next several years.

How Well Is the Organization Collecting on Pledges and Invoices?

The financial books probably record a good number of pledges and invoices such as tuition bills, event charges, and subscriptions, which have not yet been collected.

- What are the organization's policies on collecting and when does it declare them uncollectible?

- Are these policies being followed and are they adequate?

Does Debt Place Any Limits on the Organization?

There may be some outstanding debts.

- If forced to repay all debts at one time does the organization have enough assets which could be immediately converted to cash to pay off those debts?

If the answer is no, the organization is vulnerable to crisis and it would be worthwhile to review the financial plan to see if the resiliency of the organization can be improved.

Again, some suggestions on how to do this will be offered in Chapter 16.

Are Responsibilities Clearly Assigned?

Finally, at least once a year reconfirm who is responsible for what.

- Is it clear who is responsible for ensuring the budget ends in balance? It is common to find the roles of the board and the executive director are ambiguous in this regard.

- If the executive director is responsible, does he or she have sufficient authority to take actions during the year to maintain balance, or is board action required to change spending?

- If the board doesn't take action when the executive director requests, who then is responsible for budget balance?

- Are there specific consequences for either the board or executive director if the budget is not balanced?

- Are there specific consequences for either the board or executive director if initiatives fall behind schedule or fail to achieve their objectives?

If any of the answers to these questions are unclear, go back to Chapter 10 on board organization and be sure that all the financial roles described there are being fulfilled by specific individuals. It is better to make sure these responsibilities and accountabilities are clear during the good times, so that when the pressure is on during the bad times the organization will be able to move quickly and decisively.

15. FUNDAMENTALS OF FINANCIAL STATEMENTS

Accountants count money in two different ways: cash basis and accrual basis. Each has advantages and disadvantages. Cash is concrete; one either has it or one doesn't. In contrast, accrual accounting requires some estimating, it can be subjective, and it involves making some guesses. For example, accrual accounting records a pledge as revenue and asks the staff to estimate how much of that pledge will be paid and when. Alternatively, cash accounting records a pledge as revenue only when it is actually paid. It is good to know what pledges the organization has, but it can't pay bills with pledges. At the same time, accrual accounting records all bills as expenses when the organization receives the bills, while cash accounting doesn't record any expense until the bill is paid. When bills pile up unpaid, accrual accounting will tell about the pile while cash accounting will not.

So in a very simplified sense, think of cash accounting as a concrete report on today (checks received against pledges and checks sent out to pay bills) and accrual accounting as an estimate of your future (checks still to be received against pledges and bills still waiting to be paid).

Accrual accounting rules and reports can easily be confusing. For example, consider fundraising pledges. Once the nonprofit receives a pledge card, accrual accounting records the pledge as a revenue called a "receivable." There is no change in assets on an accrual basis when that pledge is paid in cash. And this pledge can stay on the nonprofit's accrual books for a year or so until its staff reluctantly concludes that the pledge will not be honored. If that happens, accrual accounting "writes off" the pledge, reduces receivables, lowers current year revenues, and shows a budget deficit on the nonprofit's accrual books. Under cash basis reporting, that pledge would have been meaningless financially until it was honored, and the nonprofit would have based no spending on the presumption that the pledge would be honored.

Considering these pluses and minuses, neither method of accounting should be ignored. The financial reports that are most commonly prepared follow Generally Accepted Accounting Principles (GAAP), which require accrual basis accounting. As a consequence, the financial reports board members would normally receive likely use accrual accounting. Unfortunately, accrual accounting reports can be especially confusing when trying to use them to evaluate monthly budget results.

I suggest that nonprofits consider preparing nonprofit budgets on a cash basis and track monthly revenues and expenses on a cash basis for board reports. I place this emphasis on cash because the annual financial report and audit should guarantee a good accrual reading by experts every year, but it is crucial for the board to have information on finances on a cash basis, which can be more readily understood by the generalists on the board.

This dual reporting will require additional work by the organization's financial staff, but the extra effort will help the board to make informed decisions and effectively monitor its priorities. Having multiple ways of tracking finances is not unusual. For example, for-profit companies routinely have at least two ways of tracking their finances since tax accounting and financial accounting can differ markedly.

Accrual accounting is a complex and sophisticated system for *estimating* the financial *condition* of the organization, but a board member needs reports that tell about *execution* of *budget priorities* in straightforward terms. I suggest cash for monthly budget reports because most crises emerge as cash problems, and cash reports can be more easily used to identify cash problems. Regardless of the confidence the board has in the staff to make good accrual estimates, cash is a fact that everyone can and should know.

GAAP Financial Statements

Even though cash financial reports are advantageous, GAAP financial statements remain the most common financial reports provided to board members and the public. They typically include a balance sheet and an income statement, also called a P&L, profit-and-loss statement, or statement of change in net assets. The balance sheet is akin to the statement you receive from your bank, except that it goes well beyond just loans and savings. Below is a balance sheet for an imaginary nonprofit.

Assets represent the resources available to support mission. Liabilities represent obligations that must be satisfied at some time. Current assets are monies accessible now and current liabilities are the obligations that need to be paid this year.

Comparing current assets and current liabilities is a quick test to see whether the nonprofit can easily pay its bills. For this organization, it cannot. While it has $186,106 in cash and $307,193 in invoices it has sent out (it expects to get paid for all but $40,114 of those invoices), it has $124,323 in bills it has received but has not yet paid. If it paid them now, it would have barely enough cash to pay an outstanding payroll obligation (probably some severance to a former employee). The big problem is that it has a $453,178 note from the Jones Bank that is due this year and it doesn't have enough ready assets to pay it off.

Example of a Mid-Year Balance Sheet Report

ASSETS		LIABILITIES	
CURRENT ASSETS		Accounts Payable	124,323
Cash Assets	$186,106	Payroll Liabilities	50,000
Accounts Receivable	$307,193	Note-Jones Bank	453,178
Allowance for Uncollectibles	($40,114)	**TOTAL CURRENT LIABILITIES**	**$627,501**
Store Inventory	$43,250		
Prepaid Expenses	$2,500		
TOTAL CURRENT ASSETS	**$498,935**	Equipment Lease	46,612
		Smith Loan #6	18,147
INVESTMENTS		Arcam Loan Boiler	2,825
Mutual Funds Inc.	$148,177	Tractor Lease	13,203
Community Foundation	$176,419	**TOTAL NONCURRENT LIABILITIES**	**$80,787**
Maintenance Endowment	$300,000		
Program Services Trust	$1,484,176	**UNRESTRICTED NET ASSETS**	**$844,159**
TOTAL INVESTMENTS	**$2,108,772**	Board Designated Reserves	176,419
		Fixed Assets	$728,916
FIXED ASSETS		Other	(61,176)
Property, Plant, Equipment	$1,264,153		
Depreciation on PPE	($535,237)	**TEMPORARILY RESTRICTED NET ASSETS**	**$89,209**
TOTAL FIXED ASSETS	**$728,916**	Maintenance Endowment	15,000
		Program Services Trust	74,209
TOTAL ASSETS	**$3,336,623**		
		PERMANENTLY RESTRICTED NET ASSETS	**$1,694,967**
		Maintenance Endowment	285,000
		Program Services Trust	1,409,967

This problem leads us to look at other assets, the investments. Investments are recorded on both sides of this table. On the left are listed four categories of investments totaling $2,108,772 – more than enough to pay off a loan if they were all available for this use, but they aren't. On the right side of the table are listed three net asset classes: unrestricted, temporarily restricted, and permanently restricted. The last category should not be used this year. Yes, permanently restricted net assets make one feel well off, but the nonprofit shouldn't touch them to pay these bills because it received the monies as gifts with legal restrictions on how and when it could access the monies.

The temporarily restricted fund balances are $89,209 and the components have the same names as the permanently restricted balances: the maintenance endowment and the program services trust. Temporary restriction means that the funds are available this year but only for the purposes specified by the original donor. I will come back to this later because the staff may already be including these monies in their budget for this year.

Unrestricted net assets are large but a significant portion represents property and equipment, called fixed assets. Unrestricted means that the nonprofit can sell those assets for cash whenever it wants, but, programmatically, selling property and equipment may severely compromise mission. The board will need to discuss the merits of selling some property if necessary to pay the bank note. Board designated reserves are available monies that the board earlier decided to set aside for a specific purpose. The board can change its policy, release the designation, and use the $176,419 to help pay off the note.

Unfortunately, no money is readily available without any sale of property or change in board designation (but recall, even then, the nonprofit still has to collect on its invoices and accounts receivable if it is to turn it into available cash).

In fact, the readily available resources are $61,176 short of covering what the nonprofit already has to pay this year. Since there is no clear way to pay off the bank note, the board will need to consider reducing its spending to generate more unrestricted cash, sell property, release its designated reserves, or re-negotiate repayment of the note.

Does this sound complicated? It is and I have just scratched the surface of this balance sheet. So what about the questions that are most important to the organization's mission:

- Are we focusing our efforts on our top priorities?

- Are we accomplishing what we need to accomplish this year?

- Are we able to sustain our current level of services for the foreseeable future?

The balance sheet doesn't answer these questions very easily. It wasn't designed for board leaders or for these questions. The fact that one may find this balance sheet difficult to understand or interpret is not what is most significant; what is significant is that it is not the ideal report to use to answer the questions that are most important! If presented with a balance sheet and its significance to the nonprofit's concerns is not clear, the solution is not for board leaders to learn how to interpret a balance sheet. The solution is to get the information leaders need in a form they can understand.

The second financial statement leaders will likely receive is the P&L or operating statement. The illustration here has been formatted to show in the first column the budget which was approved for this year, in the second column an estimate five months into the fiscal year of where the staff expect to be at the end of the year, and in the third column how far off from the budget this estimate is.

Example of a Mid-Year Operating Statement

RESULTS OF OPERATIONS			
	Board Approved Budget	Projected Year-End Budget	Net Projected Change from Budget
Operational Revenue			
Fees	$314,200	$416,932	$102,732
Grants	$547,300	$463,000	($84,300)
Interest Income	$2,800	$2,100	($700)
Events	$182,700	$182,700	$0
Gifts	$113,000	$143,500	$30,500
Total Operational Revenue	**$1,160,000**	**$1,208,232**	**$48,232**
Operational Expenses			
Salaries and Benefits			
Administrative	$91,000	$91,000	$0
Direct Services	$410,800	$350,800	$60,000
Facilities Maintenance	$149,000	$189,000	($40,000)
Total Salaries and Benefits	**$650,800**	**$630,800**	**$20,000**
Non-Salaried Operations			
Administrative	$63,900	$86,500	($22,600)
Direct Services	$523,900	$477,900	$46,000
Facilities Maintenance	$55,500	$52,412	$3,088
Operating Bank Loan Interest	$8,000	$8,300	($300)
Endowment Funding	($89,209)	($89,209)	$0
Loan Payments	$4,700	$4,100	$600
Non-Routine (Other)	$26,200	$10,400	$15,800
Total Non-Salaried Operations	**$592,991**	**$550,403**	**$42,588**
Total Expenses	**$1,243,791**	**$1,181,203**	**$62,588**
Net Operating Income	**($83,791)**	**$27,029**	**$110,820**

The first thing to look at is to see whether the staff is already counting on using the temporarily restricted net assets. Under non-salaried operating expenses is the line "endowment funding" in the amount of $89,209, the full amount available. So it is clear that that money is not available to pay off the bank loan since it is already committed to paying some operating expenses. The staff has chosen to record this as an offset to expenses (that's why it is shown in parentheses, as negative numbers are often shown in financial statements). It could also have been recorded as a positive number under operational revenue.

The next thing to look at is the "bottom line", which is net operating income. The first column says that the board approved a budget with a deficit of $83,791; the second column says that the staff has estimated that the budget will now end with a surplus of $27,029. The third column says that this is an improvement of $110,820. That is a very impressive ten percent savings out of operations.

Relieved that the staff believe they have addressed the budget problem, now probe to see what has changed to improve operations by so much. The third column says that salaries and benefits for direct services are expected to be $60,000 lower than originally budgeted. Recall the $50,000 of payroll liabilities on the balance sheet and ask the staff if they really have lowered costs or are they putting off an expenditure to the next year. In any case, personnel expenses are fairly unchanged at $630,800, even with this direct services item.

Continuing to focus on non-zero items in the third column, notice that direct services spending is expected to be lower for both salary and non-salaried expenses ($60,000 and $46,000, respectively). Thus most of the overall budget savings are in the area one expects is most central to mission, direct services. Since meeting mission, goals, and priorities formed the basis for approving the budget, leadership should be concerned that the organization is underspending in this area as opposed to underspending in supporting areas like administration or facilities maintenance. In fact and unfortunately, expenses in administration and facilities maintenance are expected to be higher than budgeted.

Now turn to changes in the revenue budget. There one sees that the mix of revenues is turning out very differently than expected when the budget was put together. Fees and gifts look to be stronger than expected but grants have fallen short. Grants are usually associated with direct services. The fact that grants are lower and direct service expenditures are lower should prompt a great number of questions about whether these two changes are related and how that may impact priorities, goals, and mission.

At first glance the almost one-third improvement in fees is welcome, but its extraordinary size suggests something major is happening that was not anticipated when the budget was built. Probe this issue further to learn how likely the expected improvement is to materialize by the end of the year and to learn what the answers may suggest about how and to whom the organization is providing services this year. Are these changes consistent with your mission, priorities, and goals?

By the end of the board meeting, all board members should have formed an opinion on how certain these expected improvements are and how desirable.

Key Questions on Mission-Focused Boards

1. Does the board agenda clearly convey the purpose and significance of each meeting?

2. Is the activity with the greatest financial loss also the key mission activity?

3. Do lower mission activities achieve sufficient profitability to support the losses in the key mission activities?

4. Are financial reports simple enough to make it clear to nonfinancial experts how the organization is doing financially, how the year's top priorities are advancing, and where potential concerns may emerge?

⚜ SECTION IV ⚜

SUSTAINING MISSION: LINKING MISSION TO MONEY®

Sustainability calls for insulating service delivery from the fluctuations of the economy. That requires sufficient planning to establish long-term profitability and sufficient tools to set aside reserves in good times to be used to stabilize services through bad times. Stabilization means more than maintaining expenses, it means maintaining service quality and relevance to evolving community need. Doing that requires a carefully built sequence of "pots" of resources.

One "pot" that requires critical review is endowment. Its value to near-term sustainability is often overstated and its contribution to stability is limited or negative. Nonprofits need to review carefully the purpose for which they wish to raise endowment. If their immediate problem is liquidity, flexibility, near-term sustainability, or stability, then endowment is a poor strategic choice for fundraising.

A careful review may conclude that sustainability – near-term or long-term – may require restructuring to change programs and/or program costs. It is vital that reduction decisions be made in the context of mission priority and program effectiveness. These decisions should place community need first. Merging or going out of business should not be excluded from restructuring options. The existence of one specific organization is less important than having community needs be met.

Crises can disrupt even the best strategic plans. This section ends with guidance for how boards can best support management during crisis without usurping the authority of management.

16. TOOLS FOR SUSTAINABILITY

S ometimes, despite good planning and focused budgets, the tide can turn and the going can get very rough. In Chapters 17 and 18 I talk about how to work through the short-term and long-term issues which serious budget short-falls can present. Before that let's discuss how best to protect and sustain mission before external forces, like economic recessions or dwindling community support, create sustained budget problems.

Structural Balance and Leaning Against the Wind

I have emphasized throughout this book that sustainability and reliability are the fundamental obligations of non-profits. In this chapter, I will suggest some tools to use to fulfill those obligations.

The key to sustainability is twofold. First, the organization needs to have structural balance as discussed in Chapter 3, i.e., a mix of revenue sources and expenses that grow roughly at the same pace and scale over the course of five to ten years or a business cycle. Surpluses equal deficits over time and the current mix of programs can be supported by existing revenue sources. Some periods have surpluses and some have deficits, but the amount of surpluses is enough to support the deficits if the organization can set aside and save the surpluses until the deficits emerge.

This leads to the second key to sustainability: a nonprofit needs to have mechanisms that allow it to set aside resources during flush times so that it can sustain services during lean times.

Taking the importance of structural balance to heart, a sustainable nonprofit will have used periods of strong economic growth and flush fundraising environments to prepare itself to weather a downturn. This is of course easier said than done, especially in an urban environment with strong demands for nonprofit services, but it is critical nonetheless. Overexpansion during periods of strong economic growth is one of the primary causes of structural imbalance and short-term budget crises. As discussed in Chapter 2, a nonprofit is <u>not</u> a reliable provider of a useful community need when it expands services to an unsustainable level for a few years just to have to cut back to the former level a few years later.

Avoiding overexpansion beyond the sustainable financial capacity of a nonprofit's constituency and donors requires that some service demands must be denied even when current funding is sufficient.

I recommend highlighting this statement and taping it to the front of every nonprofit leader's desk. It sounds cruel, but it is not. One may ask how a nonprofit can have surpluses or set aside reserves when it is not meeting demand for its services. A nonprofit exists because its services are needed by someone. If those services are going to be needed five years from now, it is the board's obligation to have a plan to be able to provide those services five years from now. To do that means the nonprofit has to be able to survive a prolonged drop in its revenues.

That means that tough choices exist in flush times as well as tough times.

To survive and thrive, nonprofit leaders have to develop the courage and conviction to place a high priority on long-term sustainability when every outside pressure is pushing them to devote all current resources to short-term growth.

Six Tools to Sustain Mission During Downturns

The best groundwork for tough times is laid during the flush times. Flush times are ideal for taking the following steps to build the financial strength of the organization so that it can sustain your mission and services:

1. Reduce Debt

Flexibility is critical to survival during tough times. The unrelenting cost of debt payments will materially reduce a nonprofit's options when cash becomes short.

2. Build Unrestricted Cash Balances

A nonprofit may actually be more successful in getting institutional support because it will be perceived that it is well managed and unlikely to have a financial crisis.

3. Set up Board Designated Reserves

These reserves can be accessed only by formal board action.

4. Accumulate Restricted Reserves

The restrictions on these reserves are determined by the donor and cannot be changed. They can be specially labeled as the rainy day fund, economic stabilization fund, etc. and the restrictions should specify the circumstances when the reserve can be tapped.

5. Set up Restricted Reserves to Pay for Predictable Replacement Costs

If facilities or equipment are central to the organization's ability to maintain its service levels, set aside restricted reserves for maintenance and replacement of key assets.

6. *Build an **Unrestricted** Endowment*

Lowest on the list of stabilization techniques. They are best viewed as a source of long-term income for ten to fifty years down the road whereas the first priority is to enhance the nonprofit's ability to sustain its service and mission over the next five years.

This list of tools is analogous to the advice we are all given in managing our personal finances. One: Pay off credit card debt. Two: Establish an emergency fund of six months of expenditures. Three: Start saving for major expenditures like appliances, furniture, or vacations. Four: Start to put money into legally restricted college savings plans and retirement funds like IRA's and 401(k)'s. Five: Set aside money or buy insurance for long-term healthcare and, if one owns one's home, set aside money for major repairs and renovations. Six: Only after all the other items are taken care of, start putting money into a trust fund for the next generation.

Now let's expand on how to set up and utilize each of these.

Reduce Debt

Flexibility is critical to survival during tough times and the unrelenting cost of debt payments will materially reduce a nonprofit's options when cash becomes short. It is easiest to borrow when times are good but one needs to think ahead to how the nonprofit can handle the principal and interest payments if its revenues were reduced substantially. When facing operating deficits, it is too late to cut debt costs and the limited options available will force cuts in services. Use a multi-year financial plan to evaluate the nonprofit's ability to handle debt and sustain services during a moderate to severe downturn. If this analysis reveals that it may have problems, then go against the tide by repaying debt when the "experts" are advising to borrow more.

Build Unrestricted Cash Balances

Business-oriented people love unrestricted cash balances. Cash balances finance fluctuations in cashflow so the organization doesn't need to regularly tap bank lines of credit. They allow the nonprofit to pay bills on time even when grant, tuition, or pledge payments are delayed. A financial statement with a large unrestricted cash balance gets good marks from financial types with phrases like high current ratio, strong net current assets, good liquidity, and strong balance sheet. Moreover, nonprofits may actually be more successful in getting institutional support if they have healthy unrestricted cash balances because it will be perceived that they are well managed and unlikely to have a financial crisis. The risk to protecting a nonprofit with large unrestricted cash balances is an internal risk: nonprofit leaders need to remind themselves at budget time that this money is not "available" for spending so they can't use it to avoid saying "no" to new spending requests.

Set up Board Designated Reserves

A board designated reserve is a compromise between restricted reserves and unrestricted cash balances. Board designated reserves can be allocated only by formal board action so that the bar is set a little higher in terms of accessing that money for new spending requests. (Financial statements treat board designated reserves as unrestricted and, if the reserve is held as cash, the financial ratios will be similar to ratios with equivalent unrestricted cash balances.) Board designated reserves are useful to hold capital campaign gifts, reserves intended to stabilize services during crisis, and funds to improve or maintain services or to test new or experimental programs.

It is important to establish board policies that make it clear what the reserve is intended to be used for and how extensive agreement must be to tap the funds. For example,

- Must a request to use board designated funds be approved just by a board committee (building committees especially like to tap these reserves for capital projects)?

- Should the bar be higher and require the executive committee to approve? Unilaterally or only when requested by another committee?

- Or should the bar be still higher and require the full board to approve withdrawals from the fund?

The highest bar would require the full board to approve use of the reserve and to stipulate criteria in advance that must be met before the board would be able to grant withdrawals. Similar to cash balances, the risk of this approach is the internal risk that repeated requests to support new or unanticipated expenditures with designated reserves can potentially weaken the resolve to say no. The more the board can wrap itself with well thought out policies, the more likely it will still have these reserves to draw upon when the going gets tough.

Accumulate Restricted Reserves

Board designated reserves provide flexibility for the board to change the rules and tap the funds when necessary. After the nonprofit has accumulated reasonable levels of board designated reserves, it should consider raising the bar even further by encouraging donors to finance reserves that can be spent in their entirety but with restrictions the board cannot change regarding what the reserve can be used for.

This additional step will provide even better protection from overexpansion during flush times but will be much more accessible than donor-restricted endowments.

The restrictions on these reserves are formal; are determined when the monies are received from the donor; and cannot be changed by the board. They can be specially labeled as staff enrichment fund, public access fund, educational outreach fund, etc., and the restrictions should specify the circumstances when the reserve can be tapped.

Set up Restricted Reserves to Pay for Predictable Replacement Costs

One of the most frequent victims of tough economic times is the maintenance of buildings and equipment. Roofs don't get repaired, boilers don't get replaced, carpets get worn, phones and voicemail don't get fixed or upgraded, and computers and other equipment become outdated and more prone to breakdowns. If any of these assets are central to the organization's ability to maintain its service levels, it should consider providing for their continuous serviceability by asking donors to fund restricted reserves for maintenance and replacement of key assets. Very few boards are able to do this and I personally have seen this most often done by asking a donor of a new facility to also establish a restricted reserve to support maintenance of the new facility.

I wouldn't place this type of reserve higher in priority than unrestricted cash balances or board designated reserves. But if a nonprofit is able to build those other financial cushions and still needs more downside protection for its service levels, this replacement reserve is a responsible way to set aside money.

Build an Unrestricted Endowment

Lowest in priority on my list of stabilization techniques is the establishment of an endowment. Endowments are lowest on my list because they are best viewed as a source of long-term income for ten to fifty years down the road whereas a nonprofit's first priority is to enhance its ability to sustain its services and mission over the next five years. The previous tools can help it to do that. If a nonprofit already has healthy unrestricted cash balances, some board restricted reserves, a restricted stabilization fund, and a restricted maintenance fund, then it is time to talk about endowments.

Endowments are pools of money that are invested with the requirement that only the total investment return should be spent by the organization and that the amount of accumulated total return that is spent each year must be severely limited. These two limitations form the primary distinction between an endowment and a reserve. The first limit stipulates that the original amounts invested, called the "corpus," should be preserved over time by the organization. Any time additional gifts are added to the endowment, the corpus increases dollar for dollar. Generally the second limit on the amount spent each year is stated as a percentage of the total value of the endowment. Called the "spending rate" or the "draw," this percentage is usually five percent or less and is almost never as high as ten percent. These rules have been changed recently in most states to conform with a national model law called the Uniform Prudent Management of Institutional Funds Act (UPMIFA), so be sure to check the current state statute.

Thus, an endowment is a special reserve that is intended to last forever, in contrast to the other reserves, which allow for the entire amount to be expended.

Endowments that are also restricted as to the purposes for which the nonprofit can use the income are called restricted endowments. Restricted endowments, therefore, are reserves with three limitations: (1) limitations that the original gift (corpus) should not be spent over time, (2) limitations on how much accumulated investment return can be spent each year (draw or spending rate), and (3) limitations on what the nonprofit can spend it on (restrictions). Unrestricted or "general" endowments do not have the third limitation and allow the endowment draw to be spent on whatever priorities the organization may have. Of course, if a gift will be made only as a restricted endowment, a nonprofit should accept the gift if the restriction is consistent with the nonprofit's mission and priorities; however, the gift would be vastly more valuable to the nonprofit if it were made as an unrestricted endowment or, better, as a current gift (which the board may choose to put into one of its board designated reserves).

Endowments are viewed very positively by donors and foundations and they indeed can provide a useful source of income. Just try to make sure the endowment restrictions are focused on key services rather than on secondary items that happen to interest a particular donor. The board should work closely with its development staff to ensure that restrictions on endowment gifts are consistent with the priorities and mission of the organization. If they are not consistent, don't be misled into a false security that the endowment is helping to sustain mission.

A Cautionary Note about Endowments

The actual performance and value of endowments is widely misunderstood. Endowments are usually seen as the ultimate protection for a nonprofit. While endowments are certainly valuable, I believe they are overemphasized as a source of <u>stability</u>. Endowments have ups and downs related to the ups and downs in the investment markets.

Most organizations seek to limit these year to year changes by basing their endowment draws on a percentage of the three-year moving average of the market value of the endowment, which will change more slowly from year to year. This policy is very helpful; however, it cannot completely eliminate substantial year to year changes in the value of the annual endowment draw.

The presumption that endowments provide stability is based on the assumption that the endowment will remain strong when the nonprofit's other revenue sources may decline and that the three-year moving average draw policy will eliminate volatility. The experiences of the 2001-2002 and 2008-2010 recessions demonstrated the fallacy of these assumptions. Just as revenues, government support, and private donations were falling, nonprofits saw their endowments plummet sharply enough to cause major changes in the three-year moving average. The result was that the endowment draw dropped sharply and became yet another leg slipping out from under the nonprofits. Similarly, during the latter half of the 1990s, endowments were showing stunning growth at the same time that the other sources of nonprofit support were also growing. Many nonprofits responded by increasing their spending rate, expanding their programs, or presuming that endowments would be able to reliably support a larger portion of their services.

Stability is supported by having resources that move in opposite directions, especially with respect to the economy. The economy moves in up and down cycles, which are often called recessions and recoveries. Activities that move up when the economy moves up and which move down when the economy declines are called "procyclical." In contrast, activities that move up when the economy slows or move down when the economy expands are called "countercyclical." Stability is provided when a nonprofit has a mix of revenues that are distributed among procyclical and countercyclical sources so that declining revenue sources are offset by rising revenue sources regardless of where one is in the economic cycle. Ideally, the nonprofits' expenses will show a similar blend of procyclical and countercyclical expenses.

Unfortunately, especially for nonprofits in higher education and social services, their expenses tend to be countercyclical and their revenues procyclical, meaning that expenses rise and revenues fall when the economy sours. That makes it even more important for the nonprofit to have countercyclical revenues that can increase by enough to support these rising expenses and offset falling revenues during economic downturns. Without that balance, nonprofits get a double whammy: their expenses and demand for their services rise during a recession at the same time that many of their revenues dry up.

Endowment policy can increase or reduce the inherent procyclical behavior of endowment income but it cannot eliminate it. The board should pay careful attention to its investment policy and its effect on the cyclicality of its endowment. Key elements of policy include rules on the *draw* of income each year, the *asset allocation* of how the endowment is invested across different types of investments, the *target rate of return* for the investment portfolio, and the *investment risk* the nonprofit is willing to take to earn that rate of return.

When the economy is strong and the investment markets are rising, there can be a temptation to amend the endowment policy to allow higher draws, to permit more aggressive asset allocations, to seek higher rates of return, and to permit higher levels of risk. These amendments can undermine the very stability the endowment is attempting to provide. Remember, stability means not just to minimize declines, it also means to rein in the horse when it begins to race ahead!

The endowment is always a very tempting pot of money to tap to expand services. That temptation is strongest when the endowment doesn't appear that necessary, most often during economic expansions. How can one deny a needed expense when millions of dollars are sitting in an endowment fund? When economic expansions occur, the board needs to remind itself that its fiduciary duty is to <u>sustain services during recessions</u>. When investment markets are at their strongest, that duty may require actually reducing the draw, moving to a more conservative asset allocation, reducing the target rate of return, and reducing the amount of investment risk. Remember, long term sustainability requires surpluses during economic expansion that are set aside to internally finance deficits during economic contractions. Make sure the endowment sets aside more, not less, during those expansions.

These types of decisions require courage. Build that courage by using a multi-year financial plan and testing how resilient revenues, expenses, and endowment income might be during a harsh recession. During this exercise think the unthinkable. We all wish we had asked in 1999 or in 2007 what a 3-year simultaneous decline in the economy and investment markets would do to revenues and expenses. In expansions we want to hope that the economic rules have changed, but we must remind ourselves that the post-war period has had an economic decline in every decade, and it will probably continue that way in our lifetimes.

∾

It is critical to understand that using one or more of the financial tools I have discussed is not simply optional and "nice to do"; it is a fundamental fiduciary duty of the board. If a board neglects these duties, when tough times come and it is forced to cut services and lay off staff, it shouldn't blame the economy. It should blame its unwillingness to make the tough choices when money was available. The majority of boards fail in this duty to be tough in flush times and, when the predictable economic downturns come, the newspapers are filled with stories of nonprofits that are cutting back programs at the very time when the community needs their services most. And the nonprofits throw up their hands and say they are helpless to do otherwise. Nonsense. It may be difficult and it may be rare to do otherwise, but it is not impossible.

This list of tools to sustain mission through tough times isn't all inclusive and I encourage innovation. At the same time, know that sustainability and structural balance may require the board to take unpopular positions. Conventional notions of neither "liberal" nor "conservative" necessarily support structural balance and sustainability of services and the types of tough choices I am advocating. A liberal approach to mission may tend to build expenses to the levels supported by the most flush times with the intention of meeting every need as much as possible: Why say no when the money is available? On the other hand, a conservative approach to mission may limit expenses to the most lean times, in the belief that a rising tide lifts all boats and the market economy should enable recipients of nonprofit services to help themselves when the economy is growing. Neither view of the role of nonprofits may opt for the structurally balanced, sustainable level of services that meets the organization's mission and priorities.

The middle ground best meets the mission, and experience says that the middle ground is the most difficult to defend. It is also true that the middle ground is hard to identify since one knows one was at a peak only when starting to decline. Financial policies and multi-year financial plans are the main allies nonprofit leaders have to find that middle ground of structural balance. Anticipate and avoid overexpansion and proactively use these six tools to help sustain services through tough times.

17. CUTTING BACK STRATEGICALLY

I have talked a good deal about what a nonprofit should do during the good times so it will have some resiliency during the tough times. The reality is that no matter how well a board has prepared for the tough times, it will never get it just right. During difficult times, spending will likely still need to be cut no matter how well one has planned. Planning isn't without value, however. Be assured that the cuts would have had to be much worse if the leadership hadn't drawn in the reins earlier.

Sustainability of Mission Is the Decision-Making Crucible

When talking about spending reductions during tough times, sustainability of services must remain the prime goal. It is critical that the budget cutting process be strongly focused on mission: spending that fosters mission should be preserved as much as possible and spending for secondary purposes should be cut first.

Be wary of the easy path of arbitrary cuts: freezing or reducing salaries, canceling travel and publications, deferring maintenance, and reducing service levels are not mission-focused criteria. While cuts in these areas are probably going to have to be made, know the implications of such cuts on the nonprofit's ability to sustain services during the tough times without prolonged adverse effects when times improve.

The problem with the easy cuts is that they certainly play well to the newspapers but they may not necessarily be the appropriate cuts to best sustain mission. A board is not likely to be publicly criticized if it cancels travel and training, reduces hours or services, and freezes staff salaries, regardless of the harm they may do to the long term sustainability of mission. But the board's job is to sustain the mission. If decisions on what to cut and what not to cut are justified based on mission, the leadership will have done the right thing and should not worry about the headlines.

When times are tough, it is difficult to know how much may need to be cut back because the target seems to keep moving. No slide begins overnight, nor does it have a clear ending and beginning. The biggest danger is that the organization will be behind the curve and continue to make short-term budget decisions that in hindsight may not be the right decisions. Looking at monthly shortfalls from budget is a guaranteed way to stay behind the curve. It ensures decision-making will continue to play catch up and that leaders will continue to be surprised.

The best way to solve a problem is to look ahead to evaluate the extent of the problem. Ideally there is a multi-year financial plan which can be used to evaluate how long and how deep the problem is and how effective and long lasting some of the solutions may be.

If such a plan hasn't been developed yet, at a minimum require the staff to project the year-end revenue and expense levels, including year-end cash balances, loan balances, and reserve levels. They may have concerns about the accuracy of their estimates. Don't be so concerned about accuracy: any estimate is better than none because it compels one to ask the right questions. This look ahead approach (as opposed to waiting for monthly or quarterly budget reports to show problems after they have occurred) allows the board to have time to deliberate, avoid rash actions, and take actions early enough for meaningful spending savings to develop.

A look ahead approach works best if the board has fostered a culture of openness to inquiry and partnership with the executive director. A visible eagerness of the board to know of problems early on will enhance the ability of the organization to act before problems become crises. Creating a culture in which messengers are not punished is critical to a healthy, sustainable organization. I benefited a great deal early in my career as a budget forecaster when my boss said, "I will never fire you for telling me about a problem, but I will fire you if you don't tell me about a problem." What a favor he did for me. Do the same favor for the nonprofit's staff, and be sure to stick by that promise!

Community Need and the Decision To Continue

I have talked mostly about problems caused by economic downturns. Sometimes the problems are persistent and of such a fundamental nature that they will not be solved by an economic recovery or a temporary infusion of cash. How can one know if that's the case? One can never be certain, but telltale signs of fundamental problems are recurrent budget cuts or cash crises year after year. Here again, a multi-year financial plan can help the board to look ahead to validate the persistency of problems. Possibly there is a structural imbalance that can be solved by changing the type and mix of revenues or expenses. If, on the other hand, the problems are persistent, it is appropriate for the board to begin the difficult discussion of whether the mission is no longer important to the community.

Recall that the guiding principle for a nonprofit is how well the organization meets an important community need. There is no reason to believe that community needs don't change over time. Diminished need may be reflected by declining clientele or declining community support, as shown by reduced governmental support, diminished fundraising, or more difficulty in attracting volunteers or board members. Another way to evaluate the situation is to look at other organizations nearby that address similar missions to see if they are in similar straits. If they seem to be doing better, there may be continued community demand for and support for the mission, and the problems of the organization may be internal. First look at the financial structure of the other organization, the components and mix of its revenues and expenses. See if they can easily be duplicated for your organization. Second, look at their location, staffing, board membership. Be open-minded enough to consider that the best way to continue the mission might be to merge your organization with others with compatible missions.

If the continual struggle for the organization seems to be that demand for its services has declined, the board should discuss whether the organization has fulfilled its mission so well that the work is complete. If that is the case, declare victory and go out of business. Knowing when to fold or merge out of existence is much more difficult for nonprofits than for for-profit organizations, and it is rarer than it should be. For-profit organizations continually are created, merged, or dissolved. Community needs are not so different than demand for widgets, yet nonprofits continually revise their missions in order to keep the organization going. That is a distortion of the fiduciary duty of a board.

Don't view closing down or merging a nonprofit as a last resort. The first obligation as a nonprofit board member is to effectively meet a community need. The existence of one specific organization is less important than having those community needs met. Always keep in mind that it is possible at times that the best way to meet the community's needs is to focus resources (including board, staff, and volunteer time) on fewer nonprofit service providers.

A nonprofit thrives because it is focused on a significant community need that is not sufficiently satisfied by the government or private sector. The energy that nonprofit staffs and boards spend on changing their missions in order to adapt to the times is not the best way to utilize this precious energy. It is okay to go out of business. It is okay to start a new nonprofit to address a new need. Starting with a clean slate in a new organization can at times be better than trying to retool an old organization into a new one.

What does the community feel about its needs and the nonprofit's effectiveness in fulfilling those needs? If one hears someone say about an organization, "oh, is it still around?", the nonprofit's mission may no longer be important or its impact on the mission may no longer be effective. When that happens, it is time to consider whether the nonprofit should declare its purpose fulfilled and take steps to devote the energy and resources of the board, staff, and supporters to other more current and top priority needs of the community.

18. CUTTING BACK EXPEDITIOUSLY

So far these chapters have concentrated mainly on how a board can maintain a focus on strategy and priorities and take deliberate and considered actions. However, financial crises do occur. In this chapter, I want to talk about what an organization can do when a sudden and large event occurs that leaves it with a major financial problem that must be confronted immediately. As discussed earlier, these crises most likely will take the form of sudden cash shortages. Here are some examples of events that may require immediate action:

- A tax levy that the organization has relied on for support has been defeated at the polls. The next levy election is at least six months away.

- A major grant that the organization has relied on has been denied, delayed, or decreased significantly.

- The organization has been the unfortunate victim of a major embezzlement.

- The leadership has learned of a significant number of overdue bills or unpaid taxes that are due immediately.

The emergence of problems should not necessarily trigger greater board involvement or micromanagement. Even in crisis, helping to advise staff on strategy that deals with problems is where the board should usually stay. Remember, the board's role is to facilitate decision-making and to help the executive director and staff be successful. That means the board welcomes knowing of problems so it can help and support the executive director and staff in crafting a plan of action to resolve those problems.

Any actions board members take should be focused on helping the executive director address these critical needs:

- First, the organization needs to buy time so that it can establish control over the current situation so it does not become a passive victim of additional evolving developments.

- Second, the organization should expect to encounter more problems and it needs a way to spot them as quickly as possible.

- Third, the leadership must make sure that the fix includes changes in reporting and governance so that their ability to anticipate problems and respond in the early stages will be stronger next time.

Only if the situation becomes extreme—those actions fail, the staff fails to execute those actions, or there is a persistent lack of staff response to emerging financial and programmatic problems—should the board consider proactively engaging in formulating and executing a plan of action. A wide-ranging list of potential actions is provided at the end of this chapter.

Once a cash crisis has begun, the board needs to support the simultaneous implementation of steps designed to buy time, maintain provision of essential services, and begin a process that will restore stability to the nonprofit's policy-making and service delivery. The steps are as follows:

1. Disrupt purchasing and hiring

2. Establish and maintain close monitoring of revenues and spending

3. Determine whether temporary financing is needed until changes reach full savings potential

4. Utilize the media to maintain public awareness and support

5. Initiate analysis of why the problem became a crisis and how this can be avoided in the future.

Disrupt Purchasing and Hiring

In a crisis, the foremost priority must be to stop, or at least slow, the momentum of spending and the drain on remaining cash. Even when financial problems are well known, one must confront the human tendency to maintain the status quo, continuing to handle purchasing, hiring, and contracting in routine ways. The board must see that this routine is interrupted.

Routine spending is most effectively disrupted through immediate freezes on hiring and purchasing. The purpose of such freezes is to buy time until the staff have identified permanent spending changes and have begun implementation of those changes. At that time, all freezes should be lifted since a freeze is arbitrary and totally unfocused on mission and priorities. Any freeze must have exceptions, and the determination of exceptions is the most important decision to be made. Effective ways to slow spending are necessarily context-specific, but at least two actions should be implemented immediately:

- If the current budget increased spending across the board to cover anticipated inflation, cancel all those increases and insist that the staff stay within prior-year spending levels.

- All set asides for future payments (encumbrances) should be cancelled, and restored on a case-by-case basis only after review of the nonprofit's contractual obligations and the relative importance of the purchase to the nonprofit's service priorities.

Establish Close Monitoring of Spending and Revenues

One cannot contain a budget crisis without knowing if the disruption to spending is succeeding. That knowledge can come only through a vigilant monitoring process. It is essential that the executive director place accountability for implementing the responses to the crisis with each operational manager and not just with the staff responsible for finances. Major savings targets should have detailed implementation schedules, and specific staff members should be held accountable for achieving specific savings by pre-specified dates. The process can be effective only if the staff knows that their efforts are being monitored and that any effort to postpone or avoid the spending cuts will be identified and foiled. The board can support the executive director in this difficult effort by appointing a board member or committee to meet weekly with the executive director to assess progress and offer counsel and advice on how to keep on track.

Determine Whether Temporary Financing Is Needed

Having disrupted spending and established effective controls to make sure that spending changes are taking place, there may still be a temporary cash squeeze before all actions have achieved enough savings to allow the organization to meet its remaining expenses. This situation is more likely the more severe the crisis, or the later in the crisis when forceful action was taken. Substantial changes in revenues or spending typically require six months to a year to develop the proposals, get any necessary legal authorizations, implement the changes, and realize the necessary financial benefit. (At the simplest level, for example, the annualized savings from any increase in fees or reduction in personnel will take 12 months to reach full value.) Thus, although the budget fixes are coming up to speed, some sort of temporary financing may be necessary, ranging from a few months so the organization can meet the next few payrolls to a year or two until it can reestablish sufficient surpluses to repay the debt. This financing may need to be borrowed from banks or individuals, or, with luck, it may be available as special gifts from loyal benefactors and donors. The best luck comes when the organization has followed the advice in earlier chapters and built unrestricted cash balances, board designated reserves, or restricted reserves that it can now use for service stabilization.

Utilize the Media to Maintain Public Awareness and Support

Once the crisis was discovered, the executive director should have immediately and directly informed the board, the staff, and major supporters. Once this group is engaged the next challenge is to sustain the energy and momentum for response and change. A major tool in sustaining this response is the media. In particular, the media can be utilized to make certain that there is a wide-spread perception that a financial problem truly exists or continues to exist and that tough actions are necessary and merit support.

Unfortunately, once implementation of a reduction program begins and the abstraction of budget cuts becomes concrete reality, support for the effort can quickly erode both among the staff (who hope the crisis will go away) and among the board and major supporters (who will bear the brunt of public complaints about the service cuts and the price or fee increases). The very act of talking in the media about the problems and the solutions may provide the courage and sense of community interest that will catalyze continued support for these remedial efforts.

This suggestion is often an unpopular one, and some boards will not follow this advice because it will place them under more intense public pressure and scrutiny. But that is precisely the point: the primary objective of outreach to the media is to counter complacency, inertia, routine, and "business as usual" among the staff, the board, and major supporters of the nonprofit.

In a perfect world, the executive director and board will have already established credibility with good, responsible reporters well before the need for media attention arises. Remember that the effort to sustain commitment to fiscal repair is easily undermined by speculation, "crying wolf," and idle threats of worst-case spending cuts. These actions should be avoided at all times. Instead, contact with reporters must be dominated by facts:

- what financial problems already exist

- what service effects are known versus what effects are speculative

- what options are available and what options are not available

- what decisions have been made and what decisions have not been made

- what was the net cash loss for the month and what is its significance.

Ask Why the Problem Became a Crisis and How to Prevent It from Recurring

Once the actions above have been implemented, it is time for some reflection and reform. The board should first view the crisis as an opportunity to establish a better way to anticipate problems, since current problems developed because of failure to get ahead of them. Second, the board must identify long-term, strategic solutions and not limit itself to short-term, tactical efforts. This is difficult and involves confronting very hard choices; however, the media effort that is helping sustain support for current actions also can help to build support for discussing long-term strategic solutions, including the basic options of permanently eliminating services, introducing new or higher fees, or reducing the cost of existing services.

It is difficult to create a sense of weekly urgency for strategic fixes that may take a year or more to put in place. Early identification of critical near-term deadlines for implementation of multi-year solutions will help to connect distant goals with immediate demands for action by staff and board. One must not let the present opportunity for change and reform slip away as the memory of the financial crisis fades with time. Exploitation of the financial crisis requires thoughtful analysis of the fundamental issues that led to the hardship in the first place. For example, determine if there were persistent errors in budget estimates or financial procedures that were not corrected, or if other problems led to the crisis.

It is critical to determine if the problems are transitory or structural. A transitory problem is one whose effects are not likely to persist, such as a natural disaster, embezzlement, or a large unanticipated bill. Transitory problems allow for a solution that primarily buys time until the problem disappears on its own. In these circumstances, the board should focus reform on developing better monitoring and more effective ways to anticipate problems and take early action.

A structural problem, on the other hand, is one whose effects are likely to persist and create recurring financial difficulties. Examples of structural problems are:

- a sustained decline in the local economy and philanthropic support

- service demand growth that chronically exceeds the nonprofit's ability to expand fee income or outside support

- legal mandates or contractual rules that limit the nonprofit's ability to control costs and, of course,

- permanent changes in the level or type of federal or state grant support.

Structural problems require major changes in mission, priorities, revenue sources, or types of expenditures. If the evaluation concludes that there are structural problems, the board needs to devote significant time on its agenda for the coming year to chart a different course for the organization's future.

BUDGET BALANCING STRATEGIES

Following are some common strategies used by nonprofits to respond to budget deficits. The strategies are grouped into those that provide temporary savings and those that restructure revenues or expenditures for permanent savings. They are not presented in any particular order and the list is by no means exhaustive. No one strategy is recommended or discouraged. Each nonprofit must decide which techniques best serve its unique situation and adapt those techniques as needed.

Temporary savings to get through the crisis

- Use fund reserves or contingencies

- Sell assets no longer needed or in use

- Lease or rent out property that the nonprofit owns but currently has no plans to use

- Refinance debt

- Maximize net revenues through timely billings and aggressive pursuit of overdue grants, pledges, and other receivables

- Postpone hiring of selected positions or freeze all vacant and new positions during a specified period

- Use staff attrition to accrue payroll and benefit savings over time

- Freeze spending in controllable areas of the budget (e.g., office supplies, travel, subscriptions, capital, etc.)

- Implement across-the-board spending cuts

- Provide early retirement incentives to produce salary and benefit savings and keep the position vacant or fill it at a lower salary

- Institute a mandatory or voluntary employee furlough (e.g., unpaid leave of absence)

- Delay or cancel capital projects

- Postpone the implementation of new programs or services or provide a scaled-back version

- Update your asset inventory list to assure purchases are only for essential items

- Spread capital equipment costs over several years through lease-purchase agreements

Permanent savings to move toward structural balance

- Increase fees

- Create new service charges for user-specific services currently funded by other means

- Reduce hours of operation

- Close facilities that are receiving low use or are in need of extensive repair

- Reduce service frequency or scale back existing programs

- Establish a joint purchasing agreement with other nonprofits to take advantage of reduced prices for larger purchases

- Investigate the possibility of regional service consolidation

- Limit or reduce overtime

- Replace full-time staff with less costly part-time personnel

- Examine the duties and hours of part-time and temporary staff to determine if the positions are truly needed

- Use volunteers wherever they can reduce salary and benefit costs at a given service level

- Institute safety programs for employees to reduce claims and employee absenteeism

- Extend the useful life of equipment

- Examine departmental organization charts and employee responsibilities for possible position consolidation, transfer to needier departments, or position downgrading

- Use inexpensive employee recognition practices to generate cost-saving ideas

- Require employees to pay part of health insurance or increase the amount that employees pay

Key Questions on Sustaining Mission

1. When facing demands to expand services, do the staff rigorously evaluate the nonprofit's financial capacity to sustain that higher level of services throughout a recession?

2. Are policies and procedures in place to build reserves sufficient to fund budget deficits during economic recession so that mission-focused services can be maintained?

3. Has it been objectively demonstrated that budget reductions impact primarily the lowest mission activities?

4. When reducing expenses, has it been determined whether the savings can be temporary or whether they must be part of a permanent restructuring that is "moving the dots" in the Linking Mission to Money® Grid?

☙ SECTION V ❧

COMMUNICATION

One of the themes that I hope has been clear throughout is that finances are just another language to use to communicate the organization's goals, priorities, and activities. I have talked about how strategic plans and multi-year financial plans can help the board sustain the organization's mission, and I have talked about how the organization can build a budget in a way that steadily advances that mission. I have also discussed how the board can use financial reporting to help it stay out of micromanagement, while still monitoring closely how well its priorities are being executed. The various roles that board and staff need to fulfill and how those roles may need to adapt to crises and difficult times have also been discussed.

These chapters so far have been very focused on using financial information to enhance communication between the staff and board. It's now time to talk about using financial information to tell the organization's story to the outside world. Once again, I hope to be persuasive that it is in the organization's interest to broadcast its financial situation openly and routinely.

This notion goes against the grain for many people. When times are great they like to brag about surpluses, but when times are tough they withdraw. This situation is akin to the student who wouldn't go to her professor's office hours until she had mastered the material well enough to "ask good questions." A good chance for helpful support was lost. Similarly, many organizations veil their financial challenges unless they are forced to reveal them in capital campaigns or when newspaper headlines put them on the defensive. This is a mistake that can hamper the organization's ability to become sustainable and potentially compromise its efforts to overcome crisis.

19. INFORMING A NONPROFIT'S CONSTITUENCIES

A nonprofit that has followed the advice in the prior chapters will have already established a clear mission and goals, well-articulated priorities, and a self-confidence that its money and actions are consistent in their focus. It will be on top of problems and even be prepared to anticipate problems well in advance of crisis. This ability will put such a nonprofit in a better situation than the majority of nonprofits. Clearly explaining its revenue and expense developments, its budget situation, and its overall financial condition is to its advantage.

One should not view communicating this information to outsiders as a threat to an organization's independence, reputation, or fundraising capabilities. I encourage optimism that people will be more willing to help if they know the nonprofit's mission and its financial condition and see that its representatives are knowledgeable and forthcoming in their communications.

This is an act of courage because human nature tends to recoil at the suggestion of advertising problems, viewing it as a sign of weakness. But remember, a nonprofit is recognized as an organization that is committed to fulfilling a service that the community needs and no one else is providing. It already has the benefit of the doubt by the very existence of its nonprofit status. People already believe it is doing something that no one else has been doing or has been able to do! That reflects strength, not weakness; conviction, not reticence; generosity, not selfishness; personal commitment, not passing the buck.

Every one of a nonprofit's constituents – whether a donor, a staff member, or a service recipient – has a stake in the financial health and future of the organization. The nonprofit owes them open, objective, and understandable information. Each of them has particular needs and concerns which should be addressed in all communications. I will go through each of them and talk about what they may want to know.

Donors

Let's start with the group a nonprofit may be most nervous about, its donors and grantors. They are constantly faced with requests by "needy" organizations. While a nonprofit may see donors' resources as limitless, donors most likely get annual requests that far exceed their financial capabilities. They will always consider whether their gifts are being used effectively and with good results. In previous chapters I talked a good deal about producing reports to let the board know about the mission focus and effectiveness of the organization's spending. Share that information with donors and grantors!

Sharing information means producing financial information in the context of the community's needs, the nonprofit's mission to fulfill those needs, its goals and priorities in directing the use of funds, and its assessment and measurement of its achievements. Simply mailing an annual financial report or a federal nonprofit tax return does not meet these criteria. If the board is best served by narrative reports with supporting numbers, one can be confident that donors and grantors feel the same way. Give them the context for interpreting the numbers: need, mission, goals, priorities, and accomplishments. Not only will that make the numbers more understandable, it will also help separate this nonprofit from the dozens or thousands of other requestors.

Donors are very likely to react positively to open outreach. First, the fact that the nonprofit knows and assembles that package of information tells them that the nonprofit is as concerned about the effective use of the donor's money (indeed, all the nonprofit's money) as the donor is. Second, the information provides an effective tool for the nonprofit's advocates on the staff of the donor or grantor. For large donor or grantor organizations or government agencies, there is generally at least one staff member who is assigned to be the advocate for a particular nonprofit request. Their job is to try to get funds allocated to the applicants they support. In other words, their interests are aligned with the applicant's: they "succeed" if funds are granted to their assignees. Giving them information that is objective, complete, and understandable gives them a strong argument that funds allocated will be used effectively.

While individual major donors may not have staffs to review applications, they too are usually bombarded with requests and will be most appreciative of a nonprofit's ability to both explain and document its revenue and expense developments, its budget situation, and its overall financial condition in a concise and non-technical manner. What better proof of good management than a board that has a command of what is going on? And an emphasis on strategic direction and oversight, rather than on micromanagement, is the same emphasis a good donor will have, so a strategic approach to financial management has strengthened the effectiveness of the nonprofit's fundraisers.

My message of openness concerning the financial situation extends directly into the grant application process as well. Don't be reluctant to claim that the organization is needy at the same time as pointing out that the organization has acted responsibly to sustain its mission by accumulating reserves, endowment, or cash balances. Why would a non-profit be asking for money, or why would it be a nonprofit in the first place, if it weren't in need of donated funds? Donors and grantors will assume a nonprofit is needy, and they will likely be even more inclined to support one that has tended to its financial health.

The board should already have information produced by the staff that objectively lets the board know what the organization's needs truly are. Share that information with donors. Don't spin or edit the information. Donors will decide themselves whether the organization is more needy than other requesting organizations, so one is best off showing them the same information that board members see. Providing that same format, that same document that board members regularly see will enhance the impression that the organization is telling it like it is: no varnish, no spin, and no skeletons in the closet.

Staff

While one may see them regularly, do not assume that the staff of the organization know as much about mission, priorities, and sustainability as does the board. It is quite possible that the board's positive, sustainable, strategic perspective is hard for staff to accept given their daily experience of limitless demands for services.

Every day the staff likely see where resources are not adequate, where quality is not where it should be, and where services have to be denied even to deserving clients. They want to believe that they are getting as much support as possible; they want to believe that the board is as committed to this enterprise as they are. After all, they have staked their livelihoods on this enterprise and they see the board as just volunteers (albeit powerful ones) who come to meetings periodically.

In many ways, because staff have more at stake than the board, they deserve to know what's going on even more than the board. Yet ironically most staff don't see the reports and materials that board members see. Most likely, the organization is in the typical situation in which the staff, the people with the greatest stake in the financial health of the organization, have the least information about that financial health. This can often be the source of morale problems. If gossip and the water cooler are the main source of information about the ongoing health of the organization, how could the news they hear possibly be good?

Let them know the organization's true story: what it is able to do, what its finances are, and how it is doing as much as its finances allow. Concerned that the information will discourage the staff? Be assured that the rumor mill has gone well beyond what the facts warrant. Tell them; they have as great a right to know as the board. Have the executive director tell the organization's story in newsletters and staff meetings. Open board meetings and memos from the board are also possible ways to convey this information.

Clients and Patrons

The organization's clients or patrons are also needful of information about its financial health. This is especially so for social services organizations, which are the most likely to face the struggle of limitless need in the face of finite resources. Clients need the nonprofit's help and oftentimes it will be in the uncomfortable position of limiting or denying them services or relegating them to a waiting list. Its clients want to believe that it is tying to help them, even if they have to hear "no" more often than anyone wishes.

Let them know the same story: what the organization is able to do, what its finances are, and how it is doing as much as its resources allow. If a nonprofit has accepted that long-term sustainability should be the foundation of strategic planning and decision-making, then it will be determining the service level it can provide based on the service level it believes it can reliably sustain. Explain this to clients and patrons.

Posters, notices, or regular messages for the client contact staff to convey are all possible means of communicating mission and the plan to sustain it. These messages will encourage the client community that their time will come if they are currently on waiting lists or receiving only part of the services the organization wants them to have. At the very least, the effort will have shown that the organization believes their opinions are worthy of attention and response. If the nonprofit doesn't reach out to them, the client or patron community may conclude that the organization is limiting services because it isn't committed to them or to the mission.

The Media

The underlying message here is that a nonprofit can't lose by directly communicating to its natural constituents: its donors, grantors, staff, and clients or patrons. If they don't hear the information directly from the nonprofit, they will guess; and they may guess wrong. Nonprofits gain nothing by limiting financial communication. Nonprofits have a mission, why not let them know? Nonprofits have priorities that are consistent with mission and for which they have approved specific initiatives and allocated specific dollars; why not let them know? Nonprofits know what they accomplished in the past year and they can substantiate it with good, hard numbers; why not let them know?

But not all audiences are natural constituencies and direct communication has its limits. Communicating with the broader community is probably practical only through the news media and through news reporters. News reporters can be helpful or harmful to an organization. By telling the nonprofit's story in their own words, thereby lending a third party credibility, reporters can be enormously helpful. They can be harmful by getting a nonprofit's story wrong, eroding its credibility, or by reporting on problems in the organization with which it is not already currently dealing. Perhaps because of my many years spent in media-saturated New York City, I think reporters have a tremendous potential to help a nonprofit to share its message. Most potential damage from media coverage is fundamentally up to the nonprofit and its own performance and initiative.

Let me first state the obvious: there are good and bad reporters. Good reporters are responsible and they want to get a story right. They are the reporters with whom a nonprofit needs to become comfortable. Bad reporters are not responsible and don't care what the facts are. Unfortunately, any organization will encounter both, but an organization should deal only with the good reporters and refuse to deal with the bad. If a reporter is not likely to be objective or fair, someone on the board should promptly contact the editor directly to lay out the concerns, making it clear he is talking about the choice of reporter, not about the decision to write a story about the organization. Paying attention to bylines and talking with fellow board members and civic leaders will soon convey a sense of which reporters are "good": responsible and objective. Public relations professionals in the area will be able to identify those reporters easily and can often be helpful in ensuring that the reporters handling a nonprofit's story will be good ones.

Good reporters want their stories to be right. But don't blame the reporters for the headline. Most reporters do not get to write their own headlines—that's the editor's job—and they often end up seeing the headlines at the same time readers do. They can be just as unhappy with the headlines as the subject of the article, sometimes even more so. Reporters do write the story, including the most important line, the lead. Although good reporters are not going to serve as the nonprofit's public relations agency, they will form their opinions based on a fair hearing of the nonprofit's facts and interpretation. View an interview with a reporter as an opportunity to tell the nonprofit's story. The board should choose one person, such as the executive director or the president of the board, to be the primary point of contact with reporters. Be sure that person provides facts to bolster the organization's story and be sure that all facts can be verified from publicly available documents. A responsible reporter cannot take a nonprofit's spokesperson at his or her word no matter how respectable and honorable the spokesperson is.

Let me talk for a moment about the nonprofit's chosen spokesperson. If he is wise, he will have already assembled the necessary facts to support his views and interpretations. If he is prepared, has good data to support his statements, and has a coherent story to tell, the reporter will see him as a reliable source and maybe his story will become the reporter's story. Whether this occurs will depend on how well other information sources agree with what the spokesperson has said and whether they validate his data.

If the organization has been communicating its information and story regularly and openly with its constituencies, there will be plenty of sources who will have looked at the same data as the spokesperson has and come to the same conclusions. The corroboration they will provide to the reporter will add further credibility to the nonprofit's version of the story.

On the other hand, if the spokesperson comes across as defensive, provides vague answers, or doesn't appear open and forthcoming, be assured the reporter's story will not be the spokesperson's story. The reporter will have to produce the story without input from the nonprofit, and therefore may not get it right. Worse, the reporter may be so suspicious of the spokesperson's reticence that the reporter will conclude that the nonprofit has no credibility and that whatever it says must be wrong or misleading. This unfortunate outcome is completely within the nonprofit's control.

Say what you know, acknowledge what you don't, and never guess or hypothesize.

Offer to get back to the reporter with responses for any unanswered question. Remember, the most credible story is one that comes under the byline of a reporter. If the spokesperson knows what he is talking about and has something meaningful to say, reporters can be an important ally in getting the nonprofit's story out to the broad community, whether it is about how well things are going or about how it is acknowledging and getting its arms around its troubles.

The Internal Revenue Service and Form 990

Regardless of communications with donors, staff, clients, or reporters, there are publicly available documents that nonprofits are legally required to produce, so it is wise to approach them as external communication opportunities to portray both fact and image to the public. When the IRS gave the nonprofit its nonprofit certification the IRS imposed the requirement that the nonprofit file an annual disclosure statement called a Form 990.

The IRS Form 990 is rapidly becoming the primary source of factual financial and nonfinancial information about a nonprofit because these forms are generally available on the internet. The form provides a standardized (though not perfect) way to present the latest information about a nonprofit.

The scope of its disclosures was substantially expanded beginning in tax year 2008. It asks about governance and if the organization has whistleblower, document retention, and conflict of interest policies. It asks about procedures to determine compensation of officers and key employees. It requires the filer to distinguish between program-related expenses and other expenses. It requires the nonprofit to list the names of its board members and officers as well as the amount of time devoted by each to the organization and any compensation, benefits, and expense reimbursements paid to each of them. It also requires disclosure of the compensation paid to the organization's officers and five highest paid employees and contractors (over $100,000). It asks for a statement of the mission of the organization and what it has done (and spent) in that year to accomplish that mission. Finally, it requires a listing of major contributors and the amounts given (though the names of contributors are not publicly released).

This amounts to pretty major disclosure. View it as a significant opportunity to demonstrate that the organization knows its mission, has identified clear initiatives to accomplish that mission, and has allocated resources according to priorities.

Sadly, most boards have never seen their organization's IRS Form 990, let alone taken an active role in ensuring that their story is clearly and accurately told through this form. (The form now asks if it was provided to the board before it was filed with the IRS.) Pay attention to the Form 990 before it is filed. Be assured that potential donors, foundations, oversight agencies, and reporters will pay attention to it. If one wishes to see Form 990s for local nonprofits, log onto www.guidestar.org to view the filing of any nonprofit in the United States.

The Outside Auditor and the Audited Financial Statements

The second publicly available document that a nonprofit is required to produce, unless it is a very small nonprofit, is a financial statement audited annually by an outside accounting firm. Annual audited statements are often required if a nonprofit receives monies from government agencies or certain foundations. Even if a nonprofit isn't required to hire an outside auditor, it is a very good idea to do so, and it is money well spent.

I discussed in an earlier chapter the fact that the audited financial statement is fast becoming more arcane and less useful to board members and other users. Even so, it is still widely considered to be the primary, publicly available, financial report of an organization. It is fine if an organization chooses to distribute its audited financial statement to donors and other interested parties, but don't confuse such a mailing with the financial communication I discussed previously. Mailing the financial report (or the IRS Form 990) is a nice gesture, but it is not likely to be an effective way to communicate to the vast majority of a nonprofit's constituents.

More importantly, the board must devote part of one of its meetings each year to the acceptance of the audited financial report. Because of this duty, it is important that board members figure out how to use the meeting with the outside auditor constructively, despite its arcane nature.

The annual audit meeting is an opportunity to have the confidential advice of an outside financial expert, the auditor. The purpose of formally meeting is so that the auditor can report on what issues were encountered, if any, in reviewing the financial statements the staff has prepared. An organization will almost always get a *clean opinion*, meaning that the auditor has no hesitation in saying that its financial statements present a fair picture of its financial condition. This is a pretty low hurdle to climb over, so I always look for more when I meet with the auditor.

If the organization doesn't receive a clean opinion, the nonprofit's leaders must probe very deeply to be certain they know, and are comfortable with, the quality of the information they are receiving from the staff and that the organization's financial health is acceptable. Since a clean opinion is the normal outcome, not having such an opinion can have very adverse consequences on an organization's ability to raise or borrow funds, and by extension to sustain its mission.

I urge board members to view this meeting as their annual "stupid question" tutorial. Don't be intimidated by the financial gurus on the board. It is the duty of *all* board members to know the fiscal shape of the organization. The board should meet with the auditor and use that meeting as an opportunity to learn the "story" the auditor sees from close examination of the books. Ask the auditor to compare this year with prior years and ask the auditor how the financial situation compares with what the auditor sees in its other clients. Don't let the audit meeting become technical and uninteresting; rather approach the meeting proactively and engage all board members in a probing discussion of the effectiveness and health of the organization with an informed, sympathetic, but objective professional.

Everyone on the board should receive at least two documents from the auditor before this meeting: the audited financial statements and the management letter (there are other "representation" letters, but they concern only the audit committee.) Many staff don't like management letters and many auditors won't write a management letter unless specifically asked. The purpose of a management letter is for the auditor to step away from the formalities of the auditing format and pinpoint all the things that concerned the auditor about internal controls and management procedures, but which didn't rise to the level of formal *findings*, which are bad news. In other words, this is the stuff nonprofit leaders really want to know about. Insist that before the meeting the staff write and distribute to the board and the auditor a response to each management comment along with a timetable for management to address each concern.

A board member doesn't need to study the management letter and response in detail beforehand; the important process is for the board to hear the staff and auditor go through the letter and responses <u>together in the board's presence</u>. Don't let the staff dismiss the comments as trivial: icebergs usually show only their tips. Make staff prove the comment is trivial by addressing it expeditiously. Make sure the board finds out from the auditor <u>every</u> suggestion he has.

The last parts of every audit meeting should be two private sessions: between the board, executive director, and auditor with no other staff present, and then between the board and external auditor with the executive director absent as well. Ask the auditor these questions in whichever session is deemed most appropriate:

- Are the staff able and skillful enough for the duties they are assigned? The board has surely discussed staff qualifications in other board meetings, but this meeting offers the perspective of an outside professional who has just spent many weeks working with the financial staff on a daily basis. Add the auditor's views to the information the board already has.

- What are all the adjustments or suggestions the auditor has and what is their significance? Recall that accrual accounting uses judgments and estimates. Develop a feel for whether the judgments and estimates in the financial statements are routine or unusual, particularly in these end-of-year statements. One will generally hear that there were no "material" adjustments or disagreements with the staff's estimates.

- Is there anything now or in the next year that would lead the auditor to have serious concerns about the health or viability of the organization? Are there any questionable financial transactions between the organization and board members or staff? Avoid later surprises. If something is nagging in the auditor's mind, find out now so it can be nipped it in the bud.

- Who on the board and staff worked with the auditor during the audit and what was their level of cooperation and preparation? The auditor is the board's agent, not the executive director's, or the chief financial officer's. Expect to hear the auditor confirm that the financial staff was well prepared and worked closely and cooperatively with the auditors during their engagement. If one finds that the auditor had to assemble any of the tables (schedules) or had any type of difficulty, carefully review the accuracy and completeness of the financial reports the board has been receiving from the staff over the course of the year.

These questions may seem odd or awkward and the answers boring, but believe me, someday this meeting may tease out some news early on that will help the board to make some timely decisions that will sustain mission for many years to come.

❦

Communicating financial plans and condition with the nonprofit's six key constituencies—donors, staff, clients or patrons, media, IRS, and auditor—can be a useful tool to advance, support, and sustain mission. Just the process of preparing to communicate can help clarify the organization's goals and priorities, hopes and challenges, and needs and available resources. By telling the organization's story, nonprofit leaders will feel more confident, committed, and engaged in their roles.

Remember, a nonprofit leader's job is to make sure of four things:

1. The top priorities and initiatives are a major focus of the executive director's time and attention.

2. Key activities or initiatives in the budget are occurring in the way and on the schedule that the budget anticipated.

3. There is clear and understandable reporting on what bills have been received but not paid by the end of the month (payables), including payroll taxes, unemployment insurance, workers compensation, and retirement contributions that are owed.

4. There is clear and understandable reporting on how much cash is available now and for the next few months, and what major events could possibly occur in the coming months to make the nonprofit unable to pay future bills on time (including delays and cancellations of major pledges, grants, and other "receivables").

These are the opening tasks for each board meeting. They provide assurance that management is executing properly so that the board can devote the remainder of its time and attention to strategy, which is where the board adds most value.

Using the lessons in this book nonprofit leaders can set a strategy that aligns with mission, develop a budget and allocate resources that align with strategy, focus board time in a way that will engage and energize the board, and sustain services through recession.

The primary duty of a nonprofit is to be a reliable provider of a useful community need. With the tools of Linking Mission to Money® nonprofit leaders will be fulfilling that duty and finding nonprofit service to be rewarding and satisfying.

Key Questions on Communication

1. Can the nonprofit simply and briefly describe how its services address a key need of the community?

2. Are financial statements and the IRS Form 990 available on the nonprofit's web site?

3. Does the nonprofit regularly communicate its fiscal health to its donors and constituencies, directly and through its web site, regardless whether the news is good or bad?

4. Does the board utilize the outside auditor as an advisor on ways to improve the nonprofit's financial health and operations?

APPENDIX: DO-IT-NOW ACTION RECOMMENDATIONS

■ Governing

✓ Understand how business cycles can impact both the revenues and the expenses of your nonprofits.

✓ Determine how sensitive your nonprofit is to the health of the economy and put together a set of goals to improve your ability to sustain your mission during lean times.

✓ Understand what types and sizes of reserves are necessary to stabilize services through recessions.

✓ Create a timetable of topics for board meetings in order to create a continual board focus on identification and advancement of long-term goals.

✓ At the next meeting, ask as many questions about good budget results as you ask about unfavorable budget results. Underspending can reflect under-performance, which is not an appropriate way to save money.

✓ Have board members review and agree on their primary duties annually.

✓ Identify the 3 to 5 primary activities of the organization and estimate the principal revenues, contributions, and expenses for each activity.

✓ Make sure that the activities with lower mission priority also have smaller financial losses or larger net revenues.

✓ Review your budget to make sure you don't have "cost efficiencies" that may be undermining the mission-effectiveness of your programs.

✓ Include in each annual budget at least three special initiatives that will advance, strengthen, or sustain your mission.

✓ Prepare your meeting agendas so that the purpose and intended outcomes are clear and the focus is on discussion and decision-making.

✓ Have your finance committee or board treasurer look for excessive compensation, excessive payments, and any payments or investments not consistent with your mission. Study how this is reported in your latest IRS Form 990 filing.

✓ Identify any restrictions on gifts and assets and compare them to your top mission priorities. Take steps to prevent restrictions from diverting your nonprofit's activities from its top mission priorities.

✓ Make sure that your fundraising focuses on sustainability by first building unrestricted cash and reserves to adequate levels before focusing on endowment.

■ Planning

✓ Educate your donors and grantors on recession planning and their roles in helping you to build reserves so that you can be a reliable service provider when the next recession arrives.

✓ Put in place a process to review at least every two years how the community's needs have changed and how your service programs and mission should adapt in response to the changes.

✓ Require that any proposal to expand facilities or services specify the likelihood and future reliability of the new or expanded revenue sources that will fund it.

✓ Look at how your revenues and demand for your services have changed over the last business cycle. How vulnerable is your financial health over the business cycle?

✓ Look at your balance sheet and assess how well you are positioned to sustain services during the next economic downturn: how much cushion do you need and how long can you provide it?

✓ Make sure that you have at least one goal or objective each year that enhances the future sustainability of your services. Do you have a plan to reduce debt, accumulate unrestricted cash, or fund reserves that will enhance your ability to sustain services when lean times return?

✓ Put together a set of goals to advance your mission and a second set of goals to improve your ability to sustain your mission. Have your board adopt them and build them into a multi-year plan.

✓ Determine your need for working capital and your need for separate reserves for emergencies, new program development, and major replacement costs. Have a plan to address those needs over the next 5-10 years and follow it.

■ Managing

✓ Make sure your top priority is to have at least one initiative every year for every long-term goal.

✓ Set up a process to verify throughout the year that spending remains consistent with the priorities the board has set for the year.

✓ Create a summary of what you are doing this year to move toward your long-term goals and regularly communicate this to board members, staff, donors, clients, and patrons.

✓ Make sure you have enough resources available (current assets) to easily pay your bills that are due (current liabilities).

✓ Know what are your unrestricted net assets and whether they are board designated, fixed assets, or readily available for any purpose. Know how or whether each of the assets can be used to pay your bills that are due this year.

✓ Focus on how significant differences between actual and budgeted revenues and expenses may affect your top priorities.

✓ Always have a tickler schedule for when you expect to receive payments on major pledges and grants.

GLOSSARY

501(c)(3) see Nonprofit

Accrual basis accounting a method of accounting which records transactions when they occur. Using this method, a pledge of a gift is a transaction recorded when the pledge is made, rather than when the gift is received. A bill is a transaction for payment and is recorded when the bill is received, not paid. Thus, accrual accounting provides a window into some future cash receipts or payments. This future-looking method can require the transaction to be cancelled at a later date such as when a pledge is no longer expected to be received. Pledges over a many-year period are recorded at less than full value under accrual accounting.

Annual audit a procedure performed annually by a certified public accountant to review the organization's financial account and assure the board that the financial statements it receives provide a reasonably good picture of the financial condition of the organization. Audits do not review everything but rather look at a representative sample of transactions to see if they are properly recorded under generally accepted accounting standards. The audit provides opinion letters and a management letter detailing issues of concern to the auditor regarding the organization's operating procedures.

Annual audit meeting a meeting of the full board or the audit committee in which the external audit presents the results to the board of the annual audit. This meeting is a unique opportunity for the board to learn the views and opinions of an objective professional regarding the financial health and operations of the organization.

Asset allocation the distribution of one's investments across various categories such as equities, bonds, treasury securities, and real estate. The asset allocation is the primary determinant of the likely risks and return on investment from an investment program.

Audited statements the end-of-year financial statements of an organization that have been reviewed by an annual audit.

Balancing the budget adjusting the organization's budget so that total revenues equal total expenditures. If the organization has reserves, the adjustments can include adding to or subtracting from reserves. Revenues are difficult to adjust in the middle of a fiscal year so that most mid-year budget balancing efforts are focused on expenditure changes and reserves. When a proposed budget is being reviewed, balancing can include revenue changes such as fee increases or decreases, new fundraising efforts, and grant proposals.

Board designated reserves monies that are set aside for special purposes by board resolution. The resolution can include rules or procedures for adding to or subtracting from the reserves. These rules and procedures can be changed by the board so the financial statements of the organization record these reserves as unrestricted. Reserves are distinguished from endowments by the organization's ability to utilize the entire value of the reserve while it can use only limited portions of an endowment.

Board duties the responsibilities and tasks which the board assigns to itself, as distinguished from the responsibilities and duties of the staff. Generally board duties are limited to strategic and policy issues as opposed to operational duties. In very small nonprofits with few or no staff, board duties may combine with some staff duties, which can be problematic unless the duties are carefully documented in writing.

Board officer a member of the board who has specific responsibilities under statute or by-law. The appointment of officers satisfies legal requirements but all board members share full and equal responsibility for the organization.

Budget a plan for acquiring revenues and incurring expenses for a fiscal year. A budget can be a simple set of estimates of major categories of revenue and expenditure. A budget is most useful if it is based on a specific set of goals and tasks to be achieved during the fiscal year.

Budget balancing strategies policies and plans for adjusting revenues or expenditures, utilizing reserves, investing, or borrowing in order to have resources equal expenses in a fiscal year.

Business cycle the recurrent pattern of expansion in economic activity followed by contraction in activity. One cycle is the time period from the peak of economic activity, through recession and recovery, on to the next peak. There has not been a decade in this century or the last that did not have at least one economic recession.

Cash balances investments of an organization that are readily available at their full value. Investments that can be sold at full value within one to three months are viewed as part of cash balances. Bank accounts are considered cash if they can be liquidated without significant penalty in one to three months. A one-year certificate of deposit, for example, would not generally be considered part of cash balances.

Cash basis accounting a method of accounting which records a transaction only when cash is received or disbursed. Cash accounting uses no estimates or adjustments; however, it provides no forward-looking information, such as pledges that will be received or bills that are waiting to be paid.

Cashflow the pattern of cash receipts and expenditures during the fiscal year. Cashflow is the underpinning for having sufficient cash available to meet scheduled expenses, of which payroll and tax obligations are most significant. Positive cashflow refers to periods in which more cash is received than disbursed; negative cashflow refers to periods in which more cash goes out than comes in, reducing cash balances.

Clean opinion also referred to as an unqualified opinion in an audited statement. This boilerplate language by the external auditor is generally as follows : "In our opinion, such financial statements present fairly, in all material respects, the financial position of the Company as of June 30, 2002 and 2001 and the results of its operations, the changes in its net assets, and its cash flows for the years then ended in conformity with accounting principles generally accepted in the United States." Contrast this statement with a qualified opinion, in which the auditor cannot offer such an opinion because the statements do not "present fairly" or they are not "in conformity with accounting principles." A qualified opinion is a major red flag that something abnormal is going on and the board should delve deeply into the auditor's concerns.

Community needs a demand for services that is not completely met by the private or governmental sector. Nonprofit organizations are granted tax-exempt status as an incentive for individuals to contribute funds to the organizations that provide services to address such community needs.

Conservative budget a term often used to describe a budget that intentionally uses low revenue estimates or high expense estimates. This term is a misnomer because this approach to budgeting compromises fulfillment of the organization's mission and is therefore counter to the board's responsibility to conserve the mission.

Continuation and initiatives budget a budget approach that focuses the board's attention on the subset of activities that are intended to change or improve the organization's achievement of its goals, objectives, and mission. Budgeting of ongoing, unchanged, "continuing" activities occurs largely at the staff level only.

Continuation budget the portion of a continuation and initiatives budget that includes the ongoing, unchanged activities from the prior year.

Endowment an investment account of an organization that is intended to last in perpetuity and which allows only the total investment return to be utilized by the organization. Often the amount and timing of the use of the total return is specified by the original donor or by board resolution.

Endowment draw (see also endowment payout and target rate of return) the amount of total investment return of an endowment that is utilized by the organization in a particular year. The draw may be specified by the original donor or by board resolution. The typical draw is three to five percent of the three-year moving average of the endowment's market value.

Endowment payout (see endowment draw)

Fiduciary a person entrusted with management of, and responsibility for, assets belonging to others. Generally boards of directors of nonprofit organizations are considered to be acting as fiduciaries. A fiduciary can have personal financial liability for mismanagement of the organization. It is common for a nonprofit to indemnify board members and officers and to acquire directors and officers (D&O) insurance to protect the directors' and officers' personal wealth from liability.

Financial planning a multi-year schedule of revenues and expenses that is closely linked to the strategic plan and mission of an organization and which represents an intended approach to provide sufficient resources to sustain that mission over the time period covered by the financial plan.

Financial reports (contrast with financial statements) a set of reports that are prepared for the use of board and/or staff to represent the financial activities and condition of the organization. The most effective financial reports consist of a narrative about progress on the organization's primary goals and objectives for the year with an accompanying table or two of data on that progress.

Financial statements (contrast with financial reports) financial tables that follow the specific definitions and formats required under generally accepted accounting principles (GAAP). Financial statements (as contrasted with financial reports) can be prepared only by certified public accountants (CPAs) in order to receive an unqualified audit opinion (see clean opinion).

Financial strength the ability of an organization to command sufficient resources immediately and over the long term so that it can sustain its mission despite a series of unfavorable events.

Forecasting a plan that assigns specific levels of revenues and expenses to future years. The most important characteristic of a good forecast is that the plan is based on a series of events and activities that are compatible and mutually consistent with each other. It is less important that the level of revenue or expense in any year be an accurate prediction of what revenue or expense actually turns out to be. The board should use a forecast to ascertain if its plans are mutually consistent with each other and whether the plans result in a series of outcomes that are consistent with the mission and priorities of the board.

Initiative a special project that is proposed in a budget to advance a specific goal or objective. An initiative has a specific timetable, set of desired outcomes, and list of required resources that can be easily tracked and managed over the course of the year.

Investment risk the risk that the value of an investment may decline. The cash balances of an organization generally have no investment risk, while endowment funds can have considerable investment risk. Investment risk is related to the return on investment an organization desires and to the asset allocation of the investment portfolio.

IRS Form 990 a mandatory annual filing for any tax-exempt organization except churches and those with less than $25,000 of annual revenues. The form reports on achievement of the organization's mission, allocation of expenditures to each aspect of mission, gifts from major donors, as well as payments to staff, board members, and major vendors and consultants. Widely available on the internet (www.guidestar.org), the Form 990 is increasingly becoming a primary document used by grantors and job candidates to evaluate the effectiveness and relevance of a nonprofit organization.

Macro level a term used to refer to high-level, organization-wide issues.

Micro level a term used to refer to detailed, operational issues.

Milestones in a timetable for a project or initiative, the dates on which significant stages of the project are expected to be accomplished and to be measurable. Milestones provide the board with an opportunity to inquire objectively about the progress of a project or initiative in an effective and efficient way that does not intrude on the operational role of the staff.

Model a series of equations or cells in a spreadsheet that represent the inter-relationships between various activities and their associated revenues and expenses. For example, a simple model would link change in the number of employees with change in salaries and benefits to result in the change in total payroll for the organization. The main usefulness of models is the effort in assuring that the relationships in the equations or cells are consistent with one another and with the organization's view of how the activities inter-relate.

Nonprofit an organization that is tax-exempt under the 501(c)(3)section of the Internal Revenue Service code that establishes the requirements for tax-exempt status for charitable organizations. This term is often used to refer to an organization which has tax-exempt status. Nonprofits are distinguished from for-profits by how they spend their profits, not by whether they earn profits.

Permanently restricted a class of gifts in which the donor has set unchangeable rules that limit the organization's ability to utilize the gifts. Restrictions generally specify the purpose for which monies can be spent as well as the amount of money that can be spent in any particular year. Permanently restricted gifts add to the wealth of an organization but they generally are not available for budget balancing purposes.

Profits the amount by which the revenues received from an activity exceed the expenses incurred for that same activity. It is often useful for a board to know which of its activities earn profits and which do not. Most nonprofits will have a sufficient number of profitable activities to provide sufficient monies to support their unprofitable activities and sustain the organization's mission over the years. The calculation of profit can be simplistic or complex depending on how extensively the organization wishes to allocate particular revenues and expenses across more than one activity.

Restricted a term that describes a reserve or endowment that is subject to rules concerning the purpose for which monies can be used or the amount and timing of use of those monies. Restrictions can be unchangeable by the mandate of the donor or they can be changeable at the discretion of the board.

Stability (see sustainability)

Stop-gap financing short-term temporary borrowing during a budgetary crisis that is utilized to continue timely payment of bills during a transition period in which the organization is determining and implementing actions that will return the organization to budget balance.

Strategic planning a multi-year plan which identifies goals and objectives that are necessary to sustain the mission of the organization as well as a set of projects and activities that should lead to achievement of those goals and objectives. A strategic plan should also be accompanied by a financial plan that lays out the specific resources that are needed for those activities and a plan of action to acquire those resources in a timely and reliable manner.

Structural balance a financial plan that is characterized by a stream of revenues that equals the stream of expenditures over a long period of time such as a business cycle. An organization that has structural balance is able to sustain its mission.

Sustainability a desirable quality of a service provided by a nonprofit such that the patron or client utilizing that service can know with reasonable confidence that the service will be available on a reliable basis for the foreseeable future.

Target rate of return in endowment and portfolio investment management, the desired return on investment. The target rate of return is closely related to the asset allocation and investment risk that the organization has chosen. The endowment draw is usually closely related to the target rate of return that is chosen for the endowment.

Temporarily restricted a term that refers to monies that are expected to be available for spending in the current year. Temporarily restricted monies usually are tied to specific expenses such that when the expense occurs the monies are immediately made available to pay the expense. For example, grant monies can be temporarily restricted when the money is already in hand but the organization has not yet provided the service and incurred the expense the grant is funding.

Treasurer the officer of the board who most closely works with the staff responsible for finances and who generally chairs the finance and/or audit committees.

Unrestricted an asset that can be utilized for any purpose desired by the organization. At times the board may still choose to limit the staff's discretion on the use of some unrestricted monies, in which case the unrestricted monies are usually called board designated reserves. Unrestricted assets can be immediately available (unrestricted cash balances) or they can be limited as to the amount and time they are available (unrestricted endowment or board designated reserves).

Unrestricted cash balances assets which are immediately available for any purpose. These assets are usually invested so that there is no investment risk and therefore a lower target rate of return.

Validate execution a limited form of board oversight that seeks to ensure that a high priority activity is meeting the milestones and objectives described in the budget. This oversight occurs on a monthly or quarterly basis and is limited to the criteria for success listed in the budget. It is to be contrasted with management oversight by the staff which pays more frequent and more detailed attention to daily execution by specific staff members.

INDEX

Bold refers to definitions.